Thirty

Christian D. Bobo

authorHOUSE®

AuthorHouse™
1663 Liberty Drive
Bloomington, IN 47403
www.authorhouse.com
Phone: 1 (800) 839-8640

Published by AuthorHouse 01/20/2016

ISBN: 978-1-5049-5336-8 (sc)
ISBN: 978-1-5049-5338-2 (e)

Day Zero

Hello mighty child of God. You have the ability to be an influence and to be influenced by the presence of God. I pray as you read this book, you discover more about the person whom God called you to be. In the process of writing this book I dealt with challenges in my life that I tried to handle on my own. God is going to challenge you every day to make small changes in your life. Those small changes will be a big impact on the way you approach every day. These changes are not only in your thinking, but the way you speak and how you carry yourself as a child of God.

I don't wish any negativity on you, but I do know that God wants us to grow with him. To experience growth we are going to be faced with difficult moments, but remember the Lord has overcome it all for us. He wants you to get to a place of depending on him no matter how difficulty presents itself. Sometimes we feel that we know everything about life. The power of independence can influence us to make decisions contrary to God's word. The Bible says that our life is not our own. We can't get so caught up into; *this is my life I can do what I want. I don't need any man or women in my life to keep me happy. I'm finding myself and going to church only makes my life more difficult.* Friend let me tell you something; God has your life in the palm of his hand. He can do more for you in a day than what you can do for yourself in a lifetime.

I will address some problems that believers and non-believers struggle with. I will help you on how to overcome those issues. The world views the church as big hypocrites because we sin just like everyone else. Our job isn't to judge the world for their sin because we all sin. God called us to be the light of the world. Have you ever needed a flashlight in a well-lit room? Light is needed in a place of darkness.

I am excited for you because you made the decision to purchase this book. I know that God is going to start doing some amazing things in your life. You might feel you're not ready to be committed to living the "Christian" life just yet because you're still young and you want to have fun. I know what it feels like to have temptations to do other things and avoid God. Even Jesus knows what temptations feel like. I am not saying it will be easy. If it were an easy way of living everyone would be perfect in this world. We are human and struggle with the flesh every day. You are in for an adventure of discovering more of your gifts and abilities to change the world. There are a lot of people who passed away and didn't finish all what God created them to do. I want all of God's people to fulfill their purpose here on earth. Nothing is impossible with God and he can do all things. I hope you are ready for a life changing experience.

One

When I was thinking of ideas how to start this book it was tough. I had to trust in the Lord and listen for wisdom. He directed me to go the way he needed me to. In the same way you may be pursuing a dream, but you don't know where to start. You're nervous and have doubts about it. If he placed that dream inside you it's there for a reason. He put everything already in you to be successful at it. You may be tired of listening to inspirational stuff or any encouraging word for that matter, but I believe this book will change the way you think of yourself. Not only will you experience a life change for yourself, but also others will see the change in you. You might think to yourself this book will be like another book of trying to give a false sense of hope. If you continue this book with that mindset then that's all it'll ever be for you. Believe as you go through this year that you will experience a more intimate relationship with Jesus Christ.

Reading this book will break down those barriers of being complacent or comfortable in life. You will get closer to the true reason of your creation. I know it feels good not struggling, but if you want to experience more of God, you are going to have to overcome difficult moments. Maybe you feel being a Christian is good enough and don't feel like working on yourself to develop a better relationship with God. Maybe you say you are living for God. If someone looked at your life right now would they see a trace of God in it? When we have dreams to accomplish we have to be careful. Those dreams can consume us to a point where we forget about Christ and focus on, me, myself and I. You may be in a season in your life where you constantly doubt if God is real. I understand because as humans we try to compare God with people. We think if God's real, *why is the pastor cheating on his wife? Why is God allowing all this disaster happen? Why do cops keep killing young men and women who are innocent?*

If you have been dealing with these thoughts I believe God wants to touch your life. He doesn't want you to look through your eyes of fear, confusion, or pain. God wants you to look with your eyes focused on him. We can be so easily distracted with things happening in our life. The chaos that is happening all around the world is designed to place fear in the hearts of people. Does God create all this chaos? Satan's mission is to kill, steal, and destroy. All the fear that has been created is by surrendering to the power of the enemy. When you deepen your relationship with Christ you will maintain a mindset of knowing God is your protector and he will not allow the enemy to prosper over you. You can wake up every morning with a peace in your heart that he has already delivered you out of the hands of the enemy.

You can never be too young or too old to dream. When you surrender to God's will, whatever you purpose in your heart, God will make it happen. Your old way of thinking will disgust you because you realize the poison that you were feeding your mind. Chasing those perverted thoughts and selfish needs don't make you a man or woman, but the wisdom of God will teach you more than what some of your friends tell you and gossip about to you over the phone or social media. When you are filled with God's love, your thinking changes. You shift from those desires that bring short life and dissatisfaction to wisdom from Christ. If you struggle with addictions to sex, smoking marijuana, pornography, lying, stealing and so much more. God can free you of it all. Are you willing to follow him?

Only God can help you overcome those issues because those are the things that hold you back from deepening a relationship with him. We feel we can control everything, but we don't possess the ability to overcome it on our own. We must submit to God, whom has freed us from the snares of sin.

I realized that if we want to experience God more in our lives, we are going to have to make a change. I am going to push you in the next 30 days to learn more about God. You may experience some struggles, but don't be discouraged because if you remain in the Lord he is faithful to hold you up. The Bible says in Psalms 34:19, "The righteous person may have many troubles, but the Lord delivers them out of them all."

We have been made righteous through Christ Jesus. When you go through challenges in life it's okay to pray for help and guidance. When you apply prayer and reading the word to your life you will have more peaceful nights of rest. I suggest after your daily reading to spend quality time in prayer. Pray to be filled with his wisdom for every decision you make in life. This is a step in the right direction and God will fill you with his wisdom, peace, love, strength and every good thing he possesses. You will experience the life he intended for you.

My prayer for you today: *Heavenly Father, I pray that your spirit will change the lives of your people and through wisdom; they will discover great things about themselves. I ask you Lord to soften the hearts of your people so they may receive you will full hearts. Amen.*

Two

Time and time again you wake up feeling depressed. You don't understanding why you're going through a difficult time in life. You know in your heart that there is more to life than a nine to five and barely paying your bills. Going to a nice restaurant to eat once a month is vacation to you. Now don't get me wrong I enjoy going to the movies and eating at a nice restaurant as much as the next person, but I know God has more for his people. I am not living a luxurious life, as a matter of fact; you may look at me and think I'm in the same boat as the next person struggling.

In the most difficult part in your life you can choose to wake up with an attitude of knowing God is working everything out on your behalf. You might be thinking right now, *well it's easy for you to say that, but I'm different and life isn't always that exciting for me.* Why isn't it? I loved the days when I was younger going to Disneyland (the happiest place on earth). I would lose sleep the night before because I knew I was going to have fun the next day at Disneyland. I know you're thinking in the back of your mind. My life isn't Disneyland and I live in reality. If your reality is full of pain, depression, and defeat it's time to change that mindset. What was the reason for Jesus dying on the cross? He died not only for our sins, but he came so that we may have life and have it more abundantly.

You have to choose to wake up and say to yourself, *what good things are God going to use for me today?* I got to a point in my life and decided I wasn't going to wake up sad or depressed. It does no good for me and it only makes my day worse when faced with more difficult moments. I wake up excited and with a purpose on my heart. I know there will be someone I come across who will need encouragement from God. When you wake up every day expecting something from God, he can't help but bless you. If you wake up angry and depressed about your situation, it only harms your blessings. When you put trust in God even in the worse seasons in your life, it brings honor and glory to him. I challenge you to not go to bed angry anymore. When you wake up with the same anger you had going to bed, I seems to control you the next day.

Being in debt isn't a sin, but it's still not fun to be in debt from credit cards, loans, or you spending money on things you shouldn't. Ask God to fill you with creative ideas or job opportunities that will help you pay off debts your debts. If you believe God can do it for you, it can happen. In the natural it seems impossible to get rid of it all, but God loves you too much to let you struggle when we please him. Sometimes you can get desperate for a need and ask God for someone to just come by and take care of it for you. It doesn't always work like this, but I didn't say it couldn't happen for you. God doesn't want to put a crutch on us on our belief system. He empowers us with the ability and wisdom to get it done. I would pray for the wisdom on how to meet my need rather than depend on someone to take care of it for me. I know God will never let me down. The formula to get your problems resolved is adding God to every difficult situation you face. He has all the answers that will develop you into a person of wisdom. No matter what problem you are going through he has already met your need if you believe.

You don't plan on running away from God when you experience trials in your life. Satan clutters your life to get you off focus. You may get blessed with a new job, but it's keeping you away from church because you know without money the needs won't get paid. I know the importance of having money to pay bills and other obligations, but we can't allow it to control our life. We can stay so busy and have a nice income coming through, but Satan doesn't mind it as long as you stay away from God. We convince ourselves that we're doing great since the family is taken care of and all my bills paid for. What about the relationship with God that's being destroyed in the process?

When you run away from God, whom are you really depending on in life? Is it God or yourself? When you depend on God you forfeit your old habits and form new ones. The new ways he has for you is gong to help you be successful the way he intended for you. I believe that God is going to start tugging at your heart to go back to him. I know you will listen because you're tired of the struggle you been dealing with for years. You can delay your time away from God. When you push faith to the side, you lose an opportunity to experience freedom from all those struggles you face spiritually, mentally, physically, and financially. Thank God for the freedom he gives us.

I want you to meditate on scriptures that help you in areas you are struggling with. If you don't own a Bible I encourage you to purchase one at your local Christian bookstore or church. The Bible app is also available for free on most smart phones today. Stop focusing on the negatives thoughts of you never being good enough or you will never measure up to someone successful. I want you to say out of your mouth.

Lord, you said to cast all my cares unto you. I send them to you right now. Fill me with direction from your Holy Spirit and guide me successfully in the purpose you created me for.

People may disagree with your dream, but God will direct your steps. He will not cause you to stumble. He will set your feet on solid ground.

Three

I hope by now you understand how important prayer is with God. It honors him when you allow your faith to operate during difficult situations in life. Your faith in God grows because you learn through each experience that you depend on him. A big key to experience his favor in life is having a willing and obedient spirit. How do I attain a willing and obedient spirit? I've tried to obey him and it never works.

To experience more of God's favor, being obedient to his word, opens up great things he can do through you and for you. I don't want you to be discouraged because you're not living right with God. I know he will give you plenty of opportunities to listen to him. It is up to us if we decide we obey him. It's one thing to want to obey and it's another thing to obey. If someone was to sale drugs and earn a living off of it, guess what? That's not God's best. It might be seen as a blessing from God, but he wants you to understand his will for your life. He desires a life for you much more than selling drugs and destroying people's lives.

If you were born into that type of environment where selling drugs is the only way, I want to say to you that it isn't the only way. Jesus is the way, the truth, and the light. You may think it's okay cause you're helping people get over their pain, but it's only hurting them even more. Jesus created life to be more than partying on the weekends. He gave us life so we don't have to go through life defeated. He desires for us to be victorious. You're reality right now may say opposite, but trust in the Lord. Don't go off of the lies Satan has been telling you your whole life.

There is another way out of your struggle and his name is Jesus Christ. God says that we have the choice of life and death, blessings and cursing. After giving us these options he suggests that we choose life. Why? We have been given gifts and abilities to do certain things for him. With those gifts he allows us to choose whether we do them for ourselves or for his kingdom. When he gives us the choice of life or death he doesn't always direct towards death as we see it. When we choose death we don't give God the room to grow in us. Therefore, living without Christ in us kills our dreams. Our health begins breaking down. Our families slowly tear apart. We will never reach a level to being all who God created us to be. That is experiencing death before you physically die. I don't know about you, but I want to be all who God created me to be.

Growing up I got hooked to the rap music. Whatever I heard, I would say. Even when I didn't know what they were saying, I would mumble the exact way they did. I didn't understand that it was slowly making an impression on my life. It held me back from developing a better relationship with Christ. Some of the most popular rap artist I wanted to be like was Drake, Jay-Z, Wiz Khalifa, Lil Wayne, or Kanye West. They were gifted and rich. I wanted exactly what they had. I wanted to be like these guys or just a day in their shoes. The amazing gifts they have to influence this world are used in a way to glorify themselves. The choice they made to live that life came with consequences that wasn't in my destiny.

In Psalms 37 the Bible explains how the believer shouldn't be envious of the wicked from their riches. Trust in the Lord because the riches he blesses you with doesn't come from the motivation of money, pride, sex and many other issues. We don't have to chase the lifestyles we see on television from rappers, pop-stars, athletes, actors and any other entertainers. Two thousand years ago we had the greatest influence that man ever seen on earth. Jesus Christ our Lord and Savior. The Lord knows what our spirit truly desires. When we seek him first he will bless us with the desires of our heart according to his glory and perfect will for our lives.

God wants his people successful and influencing this new generation. People claim to love God, but show their love towards other things besides God. A big thing now on television has been reality shows. I don't want you to get so caught up on reality shows and start to devalue your life because it can easily be done. You see the type of fun and drama they experience and secretly wish your life was that fun too. Reality shows are far from reality. You don't get a do-over or retake in your script of life. I am not saying reality shows are evil. They do no good for you when you reflect your life from theirs. They aren't to blame. It's the misguidance from the church that led people away from God.

God will meet every need in your life. Start today in the right direction and thinking about the presence of God in your life. It may have been a while since you came to God for direction in life, but if you honor him in all your ways he will direct your steps. You might ask God to help you handle a small or big problem in your life and it's okay. He will give you wisdom the way you need to receive it so that you can take the knowledge with you the rest of your life.

Ephesians 3:20 says' God can do exceedingly, abundantly; above all you can ask or think. This means you are going to experience some blessings you weren't praying for. His thoughts for us go beyond our own imagination. He's a God who knows want we want before the thought even enters into our mind. Does that fact amaze you like it does me? He knows what we will need before we get to our destination. He is preparing us for our journey before we even start. Once you decide you're tired of not living to your full potential, pray for a closer relationship with Christ.

Four

When I first decided to write this book it was a big deal for me. I secretly liked writing papers in English class, but never thought I would get the opportunity to write a book. I was working at a warehouse job in Moreno Valley, California at the time it came to me. God spoke to me in the middle of a long 8-hour shift of moving products down an assembly line. I got to a point of giving up on a better life and my dreams were slowly fading away. God knew that I needed to change my surroundings. I wasn't in a place mentally where I could grow the way he wanted me to. Even when I knew it was God speaking to me about writing this book, I questioned it. I didn't hesitate to ask, why me? He showed me through my life I was depending on my own abilities and tried so long to please other people instead satisfying the one it truly mattered to. He showed me that having a real relationship with him will open doors that my own ability and strength couldn't do.

I hope every one of you reading this has a dream or a desire to be at a better place than where you're at right now. Often we get so focused on ourselves we tend to cut off relationships we are meant to stay in contact with. He wants to use those people around us to help direct us to our destiny. Don't get me wrong. When we pursue a dream there are some people that won't be able to stick around. Some are meant to stick with you. It is through them you get the fire you need to continue that path to living out your destiny.

When we cut off relationships God builds for us to keep, we make it harder on ourselves to reach that dream. When you cut the good relationships and people who helped you along the way, you start to depend on yourself to make it happen. You ignore all the support God has placed around you. You may be aiming for that promotion on your job, getting out of debt, or land an opportunity of a lifetime, but insecurities stop you in your tracks. When you dream big, it is almost certain that fears and doubts will come.

The enemy knows that you are putting your trust more in God than yourself, so he wants to attack you through your own thoughts. Keep those encouragers in your life. Encouragers are the ones who push you when everyone else has given up on you. Encouragers are people who believe you can accomplish that dream more than you think you can. The right encouragers will help you develop your faith. You will realize you are meant for greater. It's easy to think good thoughts every day. It's another thing to speak words of truth about you and see it happen.

In Isaiah 41:10 it says, "Fear not, for I am with you, do not be dismayed, for I am your God. I will strengthen you and uphold you." When I would struggle in my faith I would question the Bible if his word applied to me or did I qualify for his blessings. I was living wrong and didn't fully live to my potential. This kind of thinking continued to keep me questioning the word of God and not fully grasping the reason why God said it. He does not want you to have fear, but to have faith. He is with you through it all and he will protect his children. God is the same yesterday, today, and forevermore. This verse in Isaiah applies to you and I right now. When you come across those fears of you not being good enough don't worry. You can now choose to meditate on his word and what he says about our victory in him. Having faith in his word gives us confidence to face any battle.

When you come against those fears, remember what the Lord says. Fear not! Now you can feel free to ask God how you can overcome that fear that he already tells you to not be afraid of. You might have fear of not being a good parent. Fear of thinking love doesn't really exist anymore. He wants you to be happily married and have a great family, but he needs you to work your faith to see it happen. I want you to take control of that fear, whether it's small or big. You don't have to live with that fear every day anymore. Take control of your negative thoughts because that could be the one thing holding you back from fulfilling your dreams. Your faith is like a muscle that needs to be worked do get bigger and stronger. If your faith doesn't get exercise than it can become weak. When you build your faith in Christ, it will cause you to make bolder steps in life. You won't make every decision based off emotions and feel bad about it. When you make a decision from now on, pray about it and ask God for wisdom. When you make that decision he will place a sudden peace on your shoulders after accepting his wisdom.

Five

Forgiveness is an issue we all struggle with. I understand it can be tough to forgive someone who hurt you in the past. They could've hurt you so bad you were never the same person from it. We often blame God for what happens to us. We choose to run away from his wisdom, but then we feel abandoned from the separation we create. Some things we go through in life can't be explained all the time, but I know that whatever Satan meant for evil, God will turn it around for your good. The intentions God has for us is to never harm us. We have free will to live. People make choices in life and all we can do is pray. Thank God he will protect us from allowing the enemy to prosper against us.

Owning up to the bad decisions we make usually point towards someone else because naturally it is easier to blame someone else. It doesn't have to come to a point of you sitting in your room alone crying asking God, *"why am I going through this" or "why are you doing this to me"?* The pain we experience isn't because God wants us to suffer from our sin, but he will use that pain to strengthen us for what he has for us down the road. God doesn't place anything on us we can't handle. Some pain feels like we cant get over it, but the pain isn't meant to stay. Women and men who have been molested or any form of abuse can feel pain like this. Maybe someone molested you and life was never the same after. You felt helpless and questioned if there is really a God.

Believe me when I say this, God did not want this to happen to you. God has given people the choice of free will. That person who decided to do that will have to answer to God. The Lord says that the Father avenges us. We don't have to go seeking for revenge. When you seek God, he will show you that you can experience a life with joy and forgive that person for what they did. I know you may not be in a position right now mentally for forgiveness and it's okay right now. God knows that it is a process to heal and it will not happen over night. Get it into your mind that you only want God to heal those wounds. Forgiveness can be the one thing holding you back from fulfilling your full potential in Christ. Some people take a short time to forgive and some take almost a lifetime. I want you to make a commitment to God to learn how to forgive as he has forgiven you of your sins. If you want to take advantage of the person who hurt you to feel your getting back, the pain will never go away for you.

Forgiveness and the love of Christ is the only thing that will free you from that pain. God wants you to surrender bitterness, envy, pride, anger, pity, jealousy and whatever feelings the flesh is controlled by over to him. You can miss out on so many blessings because you are so focused on getting back at that person who hurt you years ago. Ask God to show you how to forgive that person(s) who hurt you so you can move forward with what God has in store for you. We all have flaws and I bet each of you have caused major or minor pain to someone in your lifetime. It is not you to judge whether it was something small because the impact on that person may have been bigger than what you thought. If you say no, then just think about the pain you gave your mother during birth.

We all have made mistakes and are still making them everyday. Pray and ask God to fill you with his love and the desire to grow more with him. I know if you sincerely ask God he will start to change your heart and help you learn how to forgive that person who hurt you. He will give you time to forgive that person and you will have a release of pain you struggled with for so long. Your freedom lies in the hands of the Savior. He can show you how to forgive, but it requires your faith to believe he has already done it. Jesus says to love your neighbor. He doesn't say if they hurt you than it's okay to hate them. I know this can be tough to live by, but this is something God wants for us. He does understand the struggle of forgiving someone. He loved the people who were cursing his name at the cross. That is why we can go to him for strength to forgive that person. God has a plan for your life and it's not just to take a seat in church. He wants you to make an impact on people outside of the church and for you to fulfill your destiny.

Six

Hello child of God I hope you woke up this morning with a spirit of expectation. Have the mindset of expecting God helping you in every circumstance you face. You should be expecting God to do some big things in your life. It can be easy to be comfortable with your daily routines and it's hard to think anything different will happen for you. When you have expectation on your mind of something great happening, it motivates you to obey the word of God. When you're expecting less you don't desire to please God to your full potential. When you expect to get a promotion on your job, you don't work slower and come in late. You show up on time. You continue to work hard as you should since the beginning.

You might be expecting to start a family soon. Planning for marriage is no joke. Expect anything and everything is something I got use to when planning for my wedding. Make sure to do the small things so you can be placed in an opportunity to meet that right person. If you are working towards having kids you are doing physically what you can to make it happen of course. Don't ignore the other needs for having kids also. Prepare for every outcome so that you are expecting the good things of God. In case something changes you know how to react from it because you are preparing yourself for a change.

You may plan to buy your first home soon, but you don't know how it's going to happen with your income. Some of you might plan to be out of debt in 5 years or less. I say some of you because there are some people who don't expect to get out of debt. Some plan on being in debt for the rest of their lives. For the people expecting to get out of debt, do all you can to get out and experience that financial freedom God has for you.

Fitness is a big must for me. I see a lot of people that are overweight in the gym and continue coming in because they have a goal they are trying to reach. They continue working out because they expect to look a certain way one day. I stay encouraged by seeing every shape in the gym because everyone in there has a goal they are trying to reach. They know it's going to be difficult, they are determined to reach their goal. Expectation for something big will change the way you live every day and will push you to see those things happen for you. On this pursuit of achieving higher expectation, you may experience some test that will challenge you mentally, physically, and even spiritually to see if truly want what you desire.

Psalms 30 says, *"weeping may stay for the night, but joy comes in the morning."* This means you may experience some hurtful times. You may not understand why it's happening to you or why can't you have this or that. When you expect the Lord to step in and take that pain away from you, his joy will overshadow that pain. When joy is present, the Lords power is being activated in your life. God can change that spirit of not being good enough or depressed. He will turn it around.

When you expect to be sad and lonely your whole life I can only guess that you will be sad and lonely the rest of your life. When you apply this same principle of expectation to the promises of God I know you will start to see the things God has already promised you. I don't want you to think little anymore because if you think small you're going to receive small. I want you to think bigger and your faith will rise to the occasion. When you are depressed about life it's hard for your expectations to be high. Get into the right mindset that God loves you and he works everything out for your good.

If you have a dream in your heart don't compare it to others and what they are pursuing. You will lose the importance of your dream. Whether your dream seems big or small to everyone else, I want you to expect every day when you wake up that God is bringing you closer to your dreams. You will one day fulfill the dreams in your heart. God says to not lean on our own understanding, but trust in him with all our hearts. In all our ways submit to him and he will make your paths straight. The path our Lord wants for us is good. He knows the way for us to go. Surrender in your thinking to not depend on your old ways. That old way of thinking got you in the slump you're in right now. You may feel your life isn't that bad. When God begins to correct your heart on things in your life, it'll give you more of an appreciation of his grace. So I challenge you to expect God to do something big in your life this week. God knows the situation you're in. He allowed it so he can bring you out of it. He has a blessing in store for you today.

Seven

Today I hope you opened this book expecting to hear a word that is going to change your life forever. If you feel lost sometimes and don't understand what God's plan for your life, don't worry because you're not alone. Often we experience times of guessing on our life. We don't know what's going to happen. Since we don't know everything, we get scared of the future. We allow fear to control our decisions and miss out on the opportunity of fulfilling our destiny.

It's crazy how much we doubt ourselves or thinking we can't do anything amazing. We think more about us failing than succeeding. You might have seen someone you know succeed in his or her dreams and you question if you're doing what God wants you to do. Working so hard toward something and not reaching that goal yet makes it harder to see it happening. We try to stay positive, but that person we know who got their blessing really didn't deserve it. If we were to put the same energy into learning what needs to be done to be successful instead of complaining why it's not happening for us, than we can discovery the gifts and talents God placed in us.

Listening to God can be difficult because he often asks us to do things that might be uncomfortable. He wants us to be happy for that friend who got a promotion that necessarily didn't deserve it. Go out of our way sometimes to talk to that person who's always depressed around you. The days of waking up feeling alone are over. Thoughts of you never getting out of the slump you're in right now will no longer rule over you. These negative thoughts are meant to defeat you. God has the power and authority to destroy the depression you are going through.

Cancer patients have increased over the last 10 years. Fear of death wants to control our lives and get us to run away from God. That fear becomes so big that it discredits the power of God. I never had cancer before. I believe I am healed from any disease that comes against me, but even something like cancer; God wants you to praise him. Rejoice in the difficult moments. He will show his glory through you and heal you from that disease. When you experience tough times in life your actions will prove how much your faith is in God. I know the physical evidence of your current situation may not be where you want it to be. When you believe you are healed through Jesus, his miracle working power will grow in you. Your healing is one-step of faith away. You must keep God first in everything that you do and allow his word to bring you out of that struggle.

In Psalm 103 the Lord shows his power and forgives all sins and heals all diseases. To be successful as a believer in Christ you have to be totally convinced that the bible is the wisdom of God and it can be counted on. You can't pick and choose from the teachings to what you feel is right and what is wrong. Going back to what God said in Psalms. He has healed us from all diseases. So if you are facing something that seems unbeatable or no cure, your faith level must rise to a higher level because God is a good God. He can do it if you believe it. God has the power to heal you. If you don't believe he has healed you then you'll experience more of a struggle to get your healing. God wants you to receive your healing that it is already done. It may be physical sickness, emotional distress, or you feel that God hasn't been a priority in your life and you want him to heal that need.

Every day you wake up I want you to be encouraged by the Word of God. I don't want you to depend on anyone for your breakthrough other than God. He will bring the people into your life that will help you be a success, but without God directing you it will be more difficult or impossible to reach your destination. There are a lot of successful people that make a living on selling false hope. From disease to depression, God can take care of it all. We should have the urge to run away from death and towards God. You should want to experience a healthy and enjoyable life. Seek God today in the midst of your struggle and watch how his love brings you out of that storm into a brighter day.

Eight

It is time to separate yourself from the people who have held you back from experiencing the life God intended for you. I heard a great word from a pastor and he spoke about surrounding yourself with people God place in your life or also called *your circle*. One test you can do when hanging around your friends or even someone you're dating to start a conversation about God. Talk about how Jesus is important in your life and having a relationship is key to your spiritual growth. People that aren't connected to the plan God has for your life usually don't respond well to your choice of topic. Once you start to speak about God you will see a change in their attitude. They will either get offensive or submissive to the conversation.

Being offensive is someone who likes to argue about why they think God doesn't exist or why God allows so much evil to happen on this earth. You have to be secure in your faith to not allow doubt to enter in your life. The submissive person is more ready to openly talk about God and the relationship they have with him. None of us are perfect in this earth and I think the world see's believers as hypocrites. I know you hear the rumors and jokes about Christianity that make you question if it's real or not.

Romans 6:4 say that God has given you a new life. This verse means the sinful life we had before Christ is no longer counted against us. We no longer live by the standards of this world, but we can live according to God's word now. Our past sins don't hold us back from God's grace. Living in sin without God doesn't seem that bad because you don't feel guilty of the things you do. Once you turn your life to God, he begins to work on you and develop you into the person he needs you to become. It's hard to develop your faith when you're living in the world doing what the world does.

Our spirit is designed to connect to God's wisdom, but if we choose to live away from him it's impossible to please our Creator. If you are facing this trouble believe me when I say, you are not the only one facing a spiritual battle. If you feel God tugging at your heart about an issue it would be best for you to listen to him because he has the ability to change your life around and make it better. Don't you want to have a great relationship with the one who created you and experience a life full of his blessings? It can be hard to understand the concept of us being spiritual beings in flesh. The importance of our connection with God can't be stressed enough. You can be happy in life and not have a relationship with God, but what I am saying is that you won't fulfill everything he had in his plan for you. When your focus is off God, that ambition to achieve a certain life isn't encouraged by his word, but by flesh. Don't be discouraged by today's message you're reading, but encouraged because you know now what you need to do to experience a life of fulfillment.

God doesn't want you to be free in heaven and struggled on earth. He wants you to be free here on earth and not be controlled by the circumstances that have infected your relationship with him. God says that his will is going to be done on earth as it is in heaven. If there is peace and prosperity in heaven, he wants you to have peace and prosperity here on earth. Proverbs 3 helps me understand that I can trust in him no matter how tough life gets. I believe God is bringing you to new places you never experienced before. I know he will speak to you. When you listen and obey him you will see his favor on your life like never before.

Nine

I want you to start today with a confession that is going to change the way you wake up every morning. It is going to change your way of thinking on how you live every day and not hold back from obeying God no matter how difficult it may seem. I believe as you confess it God will begin to make a transformation in your life. Read this part aloud and say:

Heavenly Father, I submit my ways to you. I am looking for an opportunity to be a blessing to someone today.

I don't want you to confess this just for today, but use this every day you wake up. There will be days you don't feel like being bothered. Thank God he has given you strength to overcome any problem you face. I know when I am not in the mood to be bothered people can see it on my face. If you have an attitude of whatever situation you're facing just remember someone has had it worse than you. I know you feel like once you're in your bad mood the world revolves around you. You want everyone to leave you alone and not bug you about why you are feeling so bad. If you have an attitude of no matter how you feel you know Jesus loves you and he wants the best for you, it'll open up more opportunities to be a blessing to people.

If you know someone who has an attitude every day and it bothers you just speaking to them, share the love of Christ with them. Smack them up the side of the head with a Bible to get the touch of God on their life. I am just kidding please don't go around smacking people up the head with the word. If I were to do that it'll be a lot of people with headaches around me. If you don't know anyone you might be that person that needs that good smack. I know if you truly want to be a blessing to someone, God will bring the people to you. There are so many people who are hurting and in need of the power of God in their life. You can't be like every one else and complain all the time about how hard your day is going or the boss just won't give you a break. I mean lets face it life can be tough sometimes and more than often for a few of us. God created us to rise above our problems and live in faith.

The problem I believe is that some of us don't have faith. When we focus on God more than the problems we go through, his power will supernaturally begin to shift on our behalf. I know what your thinking. How am I going to just leave it to God when I can't stop thinking about it? That's the beauty of our relationship with God that he wants you to have with him. He wants you to depend on him no matter how big the situation. When we face tough times we are also challenged in our faith because it will show how much we really believe our Lord can bring us out of our problem. In the midst of the battle, victory awaits.

You dealt with serious problems in your life a certain way before, but did you believe the Lord would deliver you? Did you think that it's only going to get worse? Did you worry about it every day losing sleep? Were you angry towards your family because you didn't know how it was going to play out? God doesn't want you to react in fear. Trust that you can keep your confidence in the Lord. You can depend on him until your last breathe because he cares for you. He will turn that situation around for you. Keep a cheerful spirit. Trust that he has already taken care of that problem for you. Once you know more of his word you will know the truths of the struggles you face. I compare struggles with a hill I choose to run up. When I get closer to the top it gets harder. I keep pushing through that moment when my legs want to give out because I know I will reach the top.

When you expect to be a blessing to someone even in the midst of your problems God will help bring people in your life that will be a fix to what you are going through. I find it difficult sometimes to pray for others when I'm focusing on all the issues I'm dealing with. When you know that all your needs are met your focus changes. You don't complain about your situation like you use to. You will have more peace in those difficult moments.

Ten

The ways of the righteous lead to prosperity. The word says we have been made righteous through Christ Jesus our Lord. We are no longer slaves to sin. God has given us the power and authority to overcome temptation. Some people may think temptation involves just sex, but temptation is something more than that. Temptation persuades us to do things we know or not know is wrong. I know it may seem like that is just who we are and we will never change, but you are wrong. I know we can change because the word of God says we can.

We don't have to continue living with that struggle anymore. Growing in your relationship with God will be difficult at times. It's only natural to act the way you've been for years, but as you walk through it God will influence you by his word. It can sound ridiculous, but you might have to run away from that temptation. Not meaning metaphorically either, I mean getting away from that temptation to avoid losing control. In college I would have to go out the house sometimes. I had to run away from the bad influenced like weed, sex and partying. I wasn't always smart in my decisions and made the wrong decisions, but by grace I was saved.

Starting today, I want you to make an effort of getting away from those temptations. When you make those decisions God will see that you're serious about making better choices. You may come across situations that may not be so easy to get away from, but to reach the level God needs you to it will require those steps of faith. Giving in to those temptations gives more power to the enemy for control over your thoughts. You may think it's good enough to go to church and say a prayer before dinner to have a relationship with God, but you can do more. You should want more than that. If that's what we lived for, everyone would be going to heaven.

When we surround ourselves with doubt and fear we will live out what's constantly surrounding us every day. When we surround our lives with so much unbelief, God's word isn't as noticeable in our lives. When I say noticeable I am saying you will hardly recognize God when he is speaking to you. I want you to grasp the importance of having a relationship with God. It will be hard to take direction from a person you never listen to. Yeah, it sounds ridiculous, but still wonder why God doesn't speak to us. The real question is. Are we listening?

I have tried neglecting God. I have tried doing things on my own to see if things will work out even when I disobey him. It never turned out the way I wanted. By his grace he helped me stop the cycle I was going through. You might be making decisions in your life that you know it's wrong. You tried doing the *God* thing for a while and nothing good happens for you. Life can actually get more difficult for you. It's only because God must take you through a process of getting rid of all the ways of doing life you're accustomed to. It's the same idea when people go through alcohol rehab. The idea of getting clean starts off as a good idea of course, but it's totally different when that person begins. Detoxification requires time and dedication to really be free of that alcohol addiction. Your freedom is in God.

You may have thought about God as someone who watches over you, but he is so much more than that. You may not even be a believer in Christ, but something is tugging on your heart to make a big change in your life. Your addictions or lifestyle seem so hard to break and you doubt you will ever change. Erase that out of your mind because God says anything is possible. If you believe God can change your life I know he will. I have that much confidence in God that I know he is willing and able.

God wants you to have fun and enjoy life. You have put off having a relationship with God for too long. He wants so much more for your life. Your relationship doesn't start and end at church service. Church is an opportunity to get in his presence with other believers to praise him. When you attend church it refills your tank. You can't run on empty for too long. Hearing the word in service should encourage you throughout the week, to dedicate yourself more to the way of life God desires. When I wasn't living right I was afraid to attend church sometimes. I knew if I went to service that message was going to be directly to me. The preacher could've spoke on anything. I would've felt like he was speaking to me no matter what.

The great thing living for God is it only gets better. You will face some struggles, but you will experience more victories. Today I want you to confess some truth out of your mouth. The words will not make your life perfect from now on, but it will allow the power of God to move into your life. If you desire to live for God and not yourself anymore, I hope you agree with me in these words and speak them aloud:

Dear Lord, I come to you today repenting of my sins. I have not been living for you and I desire a change. I know without you I would not be standing here today. I thank you for loving me when I didn't love you. Lord I believe you died on the cross and rose from the dead. You have given me life. I don't know you Lord, but I want to know you. I accept you into my heart so that I may live with you in eternity.

If you have confessed this and believed in your heart you have been saved. This isn't the end and now you can go back to your normal life now. I suggest you find a great church home so you are hearing the word every Sunday. Interacting with believers will help you grow in your faith. Renew your mind with the word. Surround yourself with supporters who are believers that will help you be the best God intends for you to be.

If you are a new believer or rededicated your life to God I know heaven is rejoicing right now. Whether you're in a library, house, school, or jail cell I believe God is moving on your behalf now. You are now free from the power of sin and now live in righteousness with Christ Jesus. This doesn't mean you will not have any more temptations, but it does mean that Christ lives in you now and he has the power to overcome it all. To know God's wisdom you must know who

God is by reading his word and spending time with him in prayer. I know you will experience so much freedom in your life because of the decision you just made. God will give you so many opportunities to grow with him. It is a lifetime of growth. Be encouraged by the decision you made today. Not only are you on the path of success, but of righteousness.

Eleven

There are days when I wake up and frustration hits me like of ton of bricks. I get frustrated about my life and what the future has for me. I would fear waking up because the same problems will carry on to the next day. I would wonder, why good things don't happen for me? Why I didn't get my big break to be a professional football player? I allowed envy to form in my heart because of being insecure in the gifts God placed in me.

The problem with believers today is we try to pursue a lifestyle that's going to make us look good in front of people. It's nothing wrong with having things for our enjoyment, but it can cause us to miss out on our assignment. We want life to be made easy. We come up with random numbers to win the lotto. Anything to get out of hard work we are willing to do. We see the nice car and house and want to live that way so we can have that life we see on television. The importance of why God created life is slowly diminishing in the hearts of his people.

When we pursue earthly possessions, it affects our relationship with Christ because we put those things before him. The problem is we want to try and do it backwards and get rich first then go to God and say, thank you for everything so now I am ready to serve you. It doesn't work that way. If you want to truly experience Christ moving in your life you will have to pursue him more than you pursue the money, fame, drugs, and everything else that takes you away from the relationship. I know church can be boring sometimes, but it is so worth the hour and fifteen minutes on a Sunday. We spend more time looking at clothes in stores that we don't buy than we would the house of God.

I was raised in the church. I could count the Sunday services I missed on my fingers. When I moved out the house I felt I could just relax and take some time away from church. I felt I didn't really need it. I wanted to chill and do my own thing for a little bit. I figured God wouldn't mind because he loves me anyway. I thought I had more peace away from church. The church was the one thing that helped strengthen me, but I wanted to neglect it. I hope you understand that I am not putting you down for not going to church. I want to encourage you to create room to attend church more often. Going to church every Sunday doesn't make you a saint either.

The reason for it all is to develop a relationship with Christ. I don't want to nag you about going to church because I know you heard it all. You don't like going to church anymore because the people gossip too much. Maybe someone rubbed you the wrong way at church and now you're offended. If that's all it takes to get you out church then Satan doesn't have to try that hard to get you off your game. Satan's plan is to distance you far away from the wisdom of God. The plan getting away from church doesn't seem so bad because you feel you thought of the idea. You don't try to connect not going to church as something influenced by Satan.

If you don't read your Bible or spend time in prayer, where do you get your faith? Being in the presence of the Lord invites him into your heart. Nothing is wrong with church online and I love that people who aren't able to come to church can watch online. If you choose not to go because you don't feel like it can harm your growth with Christ. It's a sacrifice sometimes to attend church for a month straight. It feels like life gets more complicated the more you go. We get challenged when we hear a word on Sunday that rubs us the wrong way. Instead of diving more into our problems we choose to run away from them. You have to get in your mind no matter how you feel you're going to get out that comfort zone. I know God speaks, but we don't always listen.

God wants you to have faith for all things. Our faith is limited when we restrict him to certain areas. We allow God in on the small issues, but stay in denial of bigger problems we face. We not only have to speak the word over our lives, but we have to live it. Faith without works is dead. When we have faith and works to prove it then God will supernaturally take control of our situations. You say you want to have a successful business, but are you giving back to the one that will provide your needs? He is the God who loves us even when we have done wrong. Once you understand his goodness you will be set free of those limitations that have been holding you back from more.

If you don't want more from God then by all means get comfortable where you're at now.

Don't settle anymore for just being comfortable where you're at because God will only move by your Faith. When you work your faith toward a goal, nothing should stop you in your tracks. By the grace of God he has given you the ability to overcome any obstacle. Let God intervene in your life today. He wants more for you now because he knows you are able to run with that dream. Don't worry he will eventually break down those walls in time. Don't give up because today's victory is just the beginning of God's goodness in your life.

Twelve

I was sitting in my room thinking one day about fears. Why do fears limit our abilities? We end up losing a great opportunity that God places in front of us because we allow the fear to take hold of us. I know you try to apply logic and statistics, but in the end fear shouldn't make your decision for you. When you aim toward a dream God requires faith. I know sometimes we analyze the situation and try to come up with excuses as to why it won't happen for you. I believe if God placed a dream in your heart then it's meant to be accomplished.

Fear isn't something God places in us. It's natural for us to have fears for problems that are bigger than us. The problem you face will be defeated when you change your mindset. Your mind puts together a scenario of how you're going to fail at it. We defeat ourselves before we even get to the problem. Fear can cause you to run away from your God given purpose and towards a mediocre life. We will eventually be with him in heaven where all things are perfect, but God wants his children to live with a purpose.

When it comes to fulfilling dreams we sometimes want to push our beliefs to the side because we feel it is going to cramp our style if we change for God. A lot of people will change for the money much easier than for God. But change is the best thing for us because that is when God steps in and shows his grace. You feel a little scared sometimes because you had some bad experiences, but keep focused on God. Jesus once said to his disciples, "*be of good cheer, it is I, do not be afraid.*" When you overcome your fears you will recognize it was Jesus all along.

If you say you don't fear anything I tip my hat to you because I face challenges almost every day. The way I handle my fear is not trying to be tough about it. I recognize the challenge, but I choose to let God take control of the fear. I think fear comes up more often than we think. It is what we do in that time of fear that shows our faith. Either we will be afraid by initiating the act of being fearful or acting in faith and overcoming that fear.

A professional boxer can't step into the ring with fear. Boxers know that a fight is as much mental as physical. At the end of the match it is always a winner and a loser. The winner may have a bloody eye and a broken rib, but they didn't give up. The winner doesn't always come out looking perfect. You have victory in life not because you are fighting, but because the Lord has already won. Stand firm in the fight. You may get some bumps and bruises along the way, but you are already a winner.

You may have been faced with a battle for years and it seems like you will never defeat it. God said that he has already won the battle for you and it is not your fight but it is his. When we are preparing to accomplish a dream and have an opportunity to fulfill it, holding back is the last thing to do. You are set free from any control from fear. Don't allow fear to control you today. When you approach something bigger than you today give God authority in your life to step in and take that weight off your shoulders.

Thirteen

There are over 7.13 billion people in the world. I sometimes think about the days of Noah and how God chose his family for a big assignment. It all started with a plan of one family. Now we have millions of families growing every day around the world. Noah and his family had a purpose and that was to go forth with God's plan and repopulate the earth because of the good God saw in Noah. Not only to repopulate, but also to keep God's plan in the hearts of his people. Sad to say in 2016 every one does not have the plan of God on their minds.

Noah was led by his dreams to proclaim the God of Heaven as Creator and Ruler of all. He obeyed God no matter how tough it looked in the natural because he understood the plan God had for him and his family. Out of the billions of people in this world how much would you say is living God's purpose for their lives?

You may have a dream to be a professional athlete, hip/hop artist, actor, or to own your own business, and the list goes on and on. Are you willing to fully obey God to see his plan for your life come alive through you? Honor God when you pursue your passions. You achieving your goals aren't to stunt on someone who doubted you or did you wrong. If you didn't know by now your dream fulfillment isn't for you to get glory, but it's for God. When we get that promotion or big break it seems we think opposite. The pride builds up in us. We are convinced that it was all us who made it happen. If it weren't for the grace of God you would be in a corner somewhere complaining about life. It's about allowing God to use that dream as a platform to spread his love in the earth. When you are faced with challenges along the way, are you thinking about giving up or quitting? If you haven't thought about giving up I don't think you're dreaming big enough.

My high school football coach told my teammates and I something interesting that stayed with me through college. He explained how our last game might be the last football game some of us play and to give 100% out on the field. It never really hit me until college because I just figured everyone would go and play in college as well. Everyone isn't equipped to do what you do. There will be some who just won't be able to stay with you on your journey.

When you are faced with tough times, realize that God wants you to depend on him to overcome those challenges you are facing. He knows that you won't be able to do it on your own. That's why he placed that dream inside you. If you have been worn down by life and feel like you can't dream anymore because it's too late, it's not. Get out of that mindset. God wants to do new things in you. If you have been dealing with pains in your body and you question if God wants you healed. Let me tell you right now,

God wants you healed! Your healing is out there. Continue believing you are already healed by the power of God. Hold on to those dreams that challenge you to be a better person.

Believe that the dream God placed in your heart is real and that he will do it for you. You will be faced with challenges even when you pursue the things of God. The amount of difficulty doesn't determine if you're obeying God or not. God is clearing up that difficult moment you are facing right now and placing you in his favor. He is your strength when you are weak. I thank God every day that he continues to encourage me to dream in spite of how it looks in the natural because I know he's been good to me. I know he will make a way some how to bring my dreams into reality. You must also believe that God has made a way for you even in that difficult moment you are in right now. Today is a new day and his favor surrounds you like a shield.

Fourteen

By now you should understand how important my relationship with God is to me. Without him, writing this book would have been impossible. Halfway writing this book I started to judge myself. I thought I wasn't good enough or qualified to be a good writer. I thought no one would want to read anything I wrote. I looked at my flaws and was discouraged because I didn't have a lot of work to show for. I continue to trust in the Lord. I had a dream and I wasn't going to let it die.

It can be hard to see as God sees sometimes because we mess up in life so much we can't imagine how God can love us when we continue to live in sin. When we focus on our flaws and imperfections it's hard to believe for that dream to happen. When we focus on our imperfections we lose focus on our vision of reaching the dream. In the process of getting off focus we potentially miss out on an opportunity for a blessing.

Finishing this book seemed too far ahead and thought I would never come up with enough material. Often times we can get so sidetracked from our goals and dreams in life because we feel God will never help us fulfill our dreams. When we feel we are getting closer to our dreams we judge ourselves more than anyone else does and make up reasons why it probably will not happen. We say to ourselves, "how can a person like me be blessed by God?" Through trial and error I was corrected in my stubborn ways of thinking. I wish I could tell you that I am perfect and don't make mistakes, but that would be a lie.

No matter how old or young we have the ability to grow in knowledge. It's up to us to choose to learn from our mistakes or continue to make the same mistakes. Lean not on your own understanding, but submit to him in all your ways. Just like the days I didn't feel good enough to write in this book, I know there are days you feel you don't deserve better. It's hard to comprehend the goodness of God. In the natural we can't do enough to earn his love. That is why through Christ Jesus you are saved and he loves you.

You might be looking for love in a different area right now for a husband or wife. You have been on so many dates you lost count. It can be the opposite and not been on a date in years. If you truly seek God to find a man or woman to marry I know he will eventually bless you when you are faithful to him. If you are applying for college and you want to get into your dream school it's okay to work harder for it. If you have a goal to get in a certain school have faith that he will open a door for you. You don't want to be unprepared for an opportunity of a lifetime.

Some friends I went to school with just don't hang around me anymore. I had a plan of reaching goals and those plans led me away to build new relationships. It might come down to leaving old relationships to accomplish new dreams. Be prepared when you go after your dreams there will be haters at your doorstep. The people aren't hatin' necessarily on you so don't take it personal. They hate on what you represent as a believer. Old friends say you've changed. People try to criticize you because of who you were in the past. Trust that God will bring people in your life to help you accomplish that dream. As you seek God in everything you do, his favor will not only open doors for you to great opportunities, but you will step into your true purpose in life.

Fifteen

I wake up some times and just don't know what to pray about. I don't know if this happened to you before, but this happens to me a lot. I know I want to pray, but I just don't know what for. Now that I understand prayer isn't just about asking God to grant my every wish, but it's more than that. Prayer is an opportunity to get closer to God. During prayer we have the opportunity to have a private session in his presence.

If we don't get our prayers answered right away we want to get it on our own. Maybe we want to live a certain status in life, but don't have the career to make it happen so we go out and buy the newest Jordan's, iPhone, or car to give the impression of success. Actuality those materialistic things don't define success. Once we get into these things it's hard to get away because we want to impress people and want them to envy us. I know if you wait on God and believe for your needs to be taken care of you won't feel the need to get those new shoes or summer outfit that is on sale just to feel accomplished. If a sale is about to start tomorrow we plan to take our paycheck and buy some new clothes or charge it to the credit card so we can fill that void in our hearts. Materialistic things can never fill the void in your life like God can.

When I was younger getting ready to move out to Oklahoma on a partial scholarship I was reminded by a pastor friend of some wisdom by God. He reminded me to not allow lustful desires take place of God in my life. I was searching for ways to fill that void, but the only thing I needed was Jesus. Even if you feel like you are going through a tough time in life you can't mask that pain with materialistic things. You think it helps and it does temporarily, but that pain will continue to creep back up unless you go to the one who can free you from that pain.

I may be only 24 years old, but I do know chasing materialistic things to cover up my pain will only make it worse. You may be older than me, but if you look at the times you experienced difficult moments, were they handled correctly? Did you ask God for strength or did you go in your wallet to spend money. Did you pray for peace and comfort or did you call up one of your friends who could hook you up with some weed and smoke your problems away? It may feel good for the moment, but that feeling of emptiness will stay. It only gets delayed, but the same problems you had before you was high will be the same right after.

My mom once preached a message called Silent Cry. This message was on how some of us go through life hurt from something in our past. We suffer from the pain and want to be healed, but it seems like no one can hear when we call for help. Christ hears your cry. Wake up every morning with joy in your heart knowing that God has freed you from that pain. If you have been dealing with physical or emotional pain, God is able to strengthen you through it. Psalms 128 says that if you obey God you will be blessed and prosperity will be yours. Prosperity according to Christ doesn't just mean having a lot of money. Prosperity is being healthy in your physical body, marriage, relationship with Christ, your finances and the list goes on and on. I can live off this scripture every day I wake up. I know the fight seems impossible to overcome right now, but you can do all things through Christ who strengthens you. Don't give up!

Sixteen

Wisdom is something we all need to survive in this world. You love God, but you keep making the same mistakes over and over again and it seems like you can't get away from it. I understand what you are going through. It's not God's intensions for you to continue making the same mistakes. God always wants you to grow and by changing your thinking and depending on his wisdom, the life he created for you will have less of a burden on you.

When I was in high school I use to hang around people who thought getting into trouble was fun. If you didn't go beat this person up or smoke weed and party you were considered a good boy. In high school no one wants likes to be considered a good boy because it's not cool. Peer pressure in school can be very challenging because it's a vulnerable time of discovering who you are as a person. Even when you are out of school the pressure to be recognized by everyone forces you to do things out of your character. We look for answers that have already been given. We aren't just called righteous, but we can live righteous through Christ Jesus.

All the looking we do for trying to find ourselves rest in the hands of our Lord.

The Wisdom of God can not only save your life, but it's the beginning of a fulfilled life. God doesn't want you making the same mistakes you did yesterday. He has given us his wisdom, which is his word so that we can grow and develop as believers. In Proverbs 4:10 it says, *"Listen, my son, accept what I say, and the years of your life will be many."* This is clearly some wisdom from God. I don't want to do anything contrary of what God is saying in this scripture. We all wish it was that easy to just obey him instantly but it is, we just choose not to. We can do it, but we choose not to because it's too much pain to obey God. Having a relationship means praying when we really don't feel like it. When we're to stay faithful to our spouse temptation weighs heavier.

If we want to fully enjoy the life God wants us to live, seeking his wisdom is the key. We hear the preachers on television talk about what God wants for us, but we still don't see it. It's not the preachers lying or God lying, it's our own will to not live in faith. Faith has to be tried first before we can say the word of God is a lie. Instead of not living the way God needs us to we choose to blame the people around us for not making us a success. If we lived broken for so long we feel God maybe doesn't want me healed.

We have to surrender ourselves to him and say, you know what God I've done it wrong for too long, show me how to obey you so I can live a long and prosperous life. I want you to seek God's wisdom every day no matter how tough it may be to say no to your old habits. He knows you're not perfect and it's not going to happen over night. Trust in him and the process of growing in your relationship. He needs you to break those bad habits so that he can create new ones. You're not doing it on your own. God has already established your footsteps. You must seek him in every stage of your life. Serve him in the good and bad times of your life. The enemy doesn't hold back when you feel you made it. He will come harder at you to throw you off your game. As you stand firm in God's word he will direct you every step of the way.

Seventeen

Feeling alone in this world is not a good feeling. Many of us wake up in the morning and feel we are all alone. This loneliness has caused you to wake up every morning depressed about life. It has stopped your passion to fulfill dreams and pursue goals. The loneliness has stopped you from loving your family or keeping in contact with close friends.

Loneliness has caused you to give up on your faith and just go through the motions of life making it through until you get old and die. I want to tell you that the loneliness that you feel isn't from God. Our Father in heaven loves us too much to put that on us. He allows it to happen because he has seen your future. He knows when you finally realize he has better for you that depression will be your testimony to his goodness.

You tried and tried at a dream and never seemed to happen so you feel that nothing else will go right for you. We depend on ourselves so much and when we fail it see like nothing else good will happen. You may be in a today that you don't like at all and wish you were somewhere else, believe me you are not alone. Trust that you will get an opportunity to get a better job or find a career you're passionate about. In the process of waiting you have to stay at your best no matter what. Keep a positive attitude.

If you are waking up every morning with joy in your heart he will begin to bring the things in your life you believe for. I understand some days you really aren't feeling it and you want to go through the day sad and feeling sorry for yourself. The route God wants to take you on only gets interrupted if you allow negativity in your life. I have been through ups and downs in my life, believed for big dreams and didn't see them happen the way I wanted them to, but I continue to wake up every morning with the joy of the Lord in my heart because I know he is faithful to honor me.

You may think I am being phony and not showing my true colors, but I am who God says I am. If God says I am blessed then it's settled, I am blessed no matter what it looks like now. If I believe, pray, and do what I need to do to see my dreams come to pass than I know if it's in his will for my life it'll happen. If you are waking up every morning feeling lonely in the world than you need to seek your true friend whom will not leave your side.

Christ lives in you today and if you seek his ways he will open your eyes more to his goodness. We may have felt lonely, but our vision will be clear when we seek him. Feeling lonely and depressed will change your mood about pursuing dreams because you feel you don't qualify. You will have more confidence in him to pursue that dream. There is nothing too big for God and he wants you to know the feeling of loneliness, bitterness, or depression is a thing of your past.

I know it can be some days you feel like crying because you don't see yourself ever getting away from feeling trapped. Just as Jesus healed the man with leprosy he is able and willing to heal you according to your faith. We must understand that it is God's will for all of us to receive his healing. When you have confidence in the Lord you don't need to get scared when things happen in your life that makes it harder. You now can say, okay God I believe that my needs are taken care of, show me what I need to do because I believe that you have already met my needs. You will live with more confidence in yourself and loneliness will be a thing of the past.

Eighteen

The power of prayer is what I had on my mind today as I woke up. As I was spending time in prayer last night I had a burst of encouragement, strength, and love that filled me. Prayer can sometimes be overlooked as something not important anymore or it's only meant before you go to bed and before good meals. If you think about it, do you really pray every time you eat, or do you only pray for big meals you feel is worth praying for?

I know I am going far into it, but if you see we can misuse prayer. Am I saying stop praying before you eat? No! Continue praying before you eat and before you go to bed, but I want you to get more of an understanding of how important prayer is to God. We are trained as a child to pray before we go to bed. It gives us comfort and peace to have a good night sleep. This isn't by accident that God gives us comfort. Just imagine spending time in prayer other than when it's time to go to bed. The type of peace and comfort God brings through prayer is life changing.

I wish prayer were so easy to just get right into it. I don't know about you, but I get easily distracted especially when something is bothering me and I don't know how to approach God. Why is it that God wants us to pray when we can easily do something else? Prayer isn't always done when it's convenient to us. Sometimes God will interrupt our plans for relaxing and watching television so that we spend time in prayer with him.

Why pray when you're about to go to the club with your friends? Why pray when you're old enough to know when you hear from God or not? We want God to be convenient for us. We want to be like a switch and turn God off until we need him again. All these thoughts come to our heads but we never want to say them out loud cause we know God wouldn't approve. I just want you to know a little something; God knows all your attentions of you not praying and why you are praying.

Don't believe the lie of not being good enough to spend time in prayer with God. You can think you're not worthy of coming to God in prayer because your life is too bad. My all-time favorite excuse of not praying is, *I just can't find time for that right now.* God wants you to have a better relationship with him. I know it's hard to start something new like spending time in prayer, but it benefits you. I wouldn't share something that I didn't believe in. I am not saying you need to spend hours in prayer, but quality time for you can be different than quality time for me. If you don't know what to pray about it's okay to ask God how to pray affectively.

In time of prayer with God he will give you a sense of understanding and peace about whatever situation you may be facing. Maybe a time in your life you prayed a lot and you loved it, but you slipped and backed off because you didn't see any of your prayers being answered. I want to encourage you to get that connection back with God because he wants to do some big things through you. I know it's been tough and trying to live like a Christian hasn't been easy, but you can't give up on prayer. It opens the door of knowledge and direction of your every day life. It can be the one thing saving you from your own destruction.

If you been praying for a family member or someone close to you to be saved and it seems like they're stuck in their ways, don't you give up on them. Continue praying for them. Believe that God is working on them. If you are uncomfortable praying with others, try praying on your own with God so you develop that confidence. Before you know it you will feel confortable praying with other people. I know it may be something you don't like to do right now, but just allow God to continue using you. God loves all his children and he wants us to feel comfortable to come to him in prayer.

Growing up if I had problems going on in my life my parents didn't want me to keep anything away from them. They encouraged me to share with them any problems I was going through. God is the same way and he wants us to come to him when we experience good and bad times. He wants us to have a great relationship with him so we can know his ways so that we can fulfill our destiny. I know he has so much in store for you.

Nineteen

I would like to first say thank you for this opportunity of seeing my growth and yours as well. I know that your dreams, goals, faith in Christ, or even your family can be difficult to be committed 100%. When you choose to obey God you are also getting the devil mad because he see's that he is losing you to the power of God that cannot be overthrown. I also don't want to scare you when I say devil, but Satan does exist and his job is to defeat us by having us give up on God. Satan tries to convince us that life is too much to be tied into a relationship with Christ. That is not the only thing he does but he ultimately doesn't want you to fulfill your true God-given purpose. He will do whatever he can to distract you.

If it means keeping you busy with work to not focus on God than he has got you where he wants you. If you think you're not in trouble because you have plenty of money and have zero debt, that isn't all the blessings God has for you. If you like to stay busy with your certain career or allo distractions to take you off focus on the main goal we are here then you will miss out on what God has for you.

You might have gone through different relationships and never found that special person. You think you need a certain type, but God will bring someone to you that will be the biggest blessing in your life. When we experience trials in our life, God's intention is not for us to feel bad because of the sin we did in the past, but to prepare us for what he has for us in the future. I have been there before. Being treated wrong for so long so you think it is God's way of paying you back for your sins.

God is a loving and forgiving God and he forgave you for all the sins. The day Jesus died and rose again was the day al our sins were forgotten. To be strong in faith is to be strong in the Lord. When you feel you're not good enough or think nothing good is ever going to happen for you, you must decide if you're going to believe it or trust in God. In the moment of the frustrating agony it's like a thick grey fog and you can't see anything good in front of you. Once you meditate on it more it seems the fog gets darker and darker until the only thing you can picture is you living in the darkness. When you live in darkness this opens up past hurts and depression cold potentially delay your blessing.

If you're not being challenged to grow in your faith every day you should make a change to have that continual growth happening. When you are at a comfortable living status and feel you know God enough and get lazy in your faith, it can potentially hurt you fulfill goals in the ladder part of your life. Being young, I can get so caught up into now, that I forget I'm going to get old one day. I use to think can enjoy my youth like I want and then obey God later.

Knowing God is a process and wasting years can delay the influence we can have on people. By the grace of God my life turned towards him at a young age. There are people who choose to go through like on autopilot and before they know it they're 50 years old. You can choose to live life the way God intended for you.

In your growth you will be tested in your faith to ensure you are reliable to what God's word says. Satan even tested Jesus multiple times. Jesus faced challenges concerning his destiny. He had the opportunity to leave the city and flee from what God needed for him to do. I thank him every day for the sacrifice that was made on the cross. When you get closer to your purpose in life you will be more challenged in your faith. You may question yourself, *am I really suppose to do this?* If God led you to it than you should go through it.

I know you might have been challenged in life and you would give up because it's just too much pressure. How many times are you going to give up on your dreams? God continues to give you opportunities and now it's time to take advantage of the position God is placing you in. No matter how dark the fog in front of you it's always a light shining. God is always with you directing through the difficult moments. Once we make it past that difficult season he can promote you to the next level. Are you ready for more from God?

Twenty

It's hard sometimes knowing you're meant for something great, but you're just not living in it right now. You think life will never get better and the "good life" is just something Kanye West raps about in the studio. For some of you if you don't know Kanye West, he made a song called the Good Life. This song was about all the materialistic things that made him desire his way of life even more. We come up with the negative thoughts about ourselves and are convinced we're not good enough.

Throughout the day we have negative and positive thoughts going through our minds. I want you to ignore the negative by focusing more on the positive. It's easy to get depressed when we look at all the negative aspects in our life. It's hard to imagine a life that we don't have yet. Sometimes the words, *like Christ* can be huge for people. We should meditate on the good thoughts of Christ because he wants to do things we couldn't do in our own ability. That is when faith kicks in. Christ now lives in us, but the problem with that is we don't want Christ to be shown in us because we are scared of what people may.

We feel God is too perfect and our lives will get boring once we commit ourselves more to God. God says that we have been made righteous through Christ and we are now purified. We can make a decision to either live for God and reap the things of his obedient children or be all about ourselves. One day I was at football practice and one of the coaches and a player were debating about if God chooses whom he wants to be saved or is it free will for us to choose. At the moment of them discussing it I couldn't answer them without anger in my tone because these two men were believers as well. God gave us the choice to choose him. God says we can choose life or death, blessings or cursing's. After this said it is suggested we choose life.

I hope by this time those two men realize the truth of God that he has given us the authority to choose him. I believe when we choose God we choose the purpose he has for our lives. Fulfilling that purpose will come challenges along the way. The life we see on television from the rap stars and actors who aren't believers aren't living the good life God intended because their souls are still slaves of sin. I am not saying they are bad people. There are good people in this world who aren't living to their full potential.

We must pursue the things of God. It doesn't say in the Bible God doesn't want us wealthy or happy and living a blessed life. We must first seek the Kingdom of God and honor him in all our ways and he will give us the desires of our heart. The problem is we get so caught up with other people we lose sight of what God really wants from us. You are meant for greater things. You may be going through hel right now, but have faith in Christ that he will turn your situation around. Don't distance yourself from God because your life is jacked up and things aren't going your way. Get closer to him so you can find out what you need to do to fulfill your purpose. Negative thinking can make or break your future.

Being a believer in Christ you must be strong in your faith to overcome the odds you face every day. People are turning away from the faith because they think it's a harsh religion to believe in a God that doesn't agree with homosexual marriage. We want to do certain things in life and if God doesn't agree we just say oh well, deal with it. God doesn't hate homosexuals. It's just a line to understanding that God wants more for us and there are ways of life that won't fully accept his wisdom. He doesn't want anything to hinder our relationship with him. He desires the best for you.

I would compare my growth with Christ like a football game. I played football most of my life and it was always a passion of mine. Playing football in middle school was exciting and fun, but there were mistakes that I made then and it was okay. I was young and it was normal to make those mistakes on the field. In high school I was expected to not make the mistakes a middle school player would make. Once I reached college I understood that football was not the same game like it was in high school. It required me to do more work on my own to be successful during the games Saturday. I realized that I wasn't playing with 17-year-old boys anymore, but passionate football players like me.

In order for me to reach my goals I had to realize that the game only gets harder as I get older. Not only does the game get harder, but also I got stronger through it. If you want to keep getting promoted to the next level you have to be willing to put in that extra work. I was the one always training on off days when people wanted to party. It seemed like they were doing better than me on the field, but I knew I couldn't give up because I was focused on my goal. No matter what it seems like right now you must know in your heart God is preparing you now for what's to come.

Twenty-One

In Romans 6:4 it says that we now have a new found life through Christ Jesus. After we choose to give our life over to Christ, why do we continue to go through the same struggles? In Romans it explains how the new life we was given by Christ defeated the power of sin in our lives. We may feel sometimes that sin controls us to do things we don't want to do. We may not want sin to control our lives, but it does when we don't allow God's way to influence our every decision. It's no way to be sinless and that is why God wants us to continue seeking him so we can grow.

I was fortunate to see one of my relatives get saved and baptized. It was a blessing to see this person coming to Christ. This person realized the life they were living wasn't honoring God in any way. This relative understood that the choice they made by being baptized now changed their life for eternity. The sins this person committed before Christ no longer matters to God, but the problem is we continue to hold on to our past mistakes. We think how can God completely forgive me of the crazy stuff I use to do? God knows you're not perfect because he made you so it won't hurt to do a little sin every now and again, right? As long as you stay happy with yourself it's okay with God. It's scary but believers think this way. We may not say it, but we show it.

Sin is in more in our lives than we think. So many of still live off the standards of Ten Commandments. We are no longer under the law because Christ has fulfilled it. This means we commit sins we don't even know of because we just aren't knowledgeable of it. There are unspoken sins that are not in the Bible and it is up to us to learn them through his wisdom because it comes back to principles of being a passionate believer.

There are some things in our lives we feel is not bad because we truly don't believe God see's it as bad. When you understand more or God, other than the 10 Commandments, you will gain knowledge. If you are living a certain lifestyle that doesn't honor God I can't judge you because I know I'm not perfect. When we focus on not sinning it arouses temptation and eventually we sin. If we focus more on the love of God in our lives, it'll slowly break us free from the power of sin.

It's not only possible to overcome those reoccurring sins in our lives, but our lessons will guide us to help someone in the same struggle we faced. Believers aren't here to condemn the non-believers. Believers in Christ are here to proclaim the Lords word until he comes. We are suppose to encourage those who not believers. We are to love them no matter what color of their skin or religion. It doesn't matter if God was black or white, but what does matter is what he did for you and I on the cross. Scientist try to prove what Jesus looked like. After it's all is said and done, Jesus died and rose again so that we may have life with him in eternity. People dislike Christianity because they feel we are the biggest hypocrites and judge everyone and talk behind their backs.

God is a loving God and even though he loves us unconditionally there is a lifestyle he wants his followers to live by and rebuke anything that isn't aligned with him. I don't want you to flee away from faith in Christ because another believer was not representing the Lord the way they should have. It can be easier to give up on church when you're going through some things in life because you see other people happier and they don't go to church. Unintentionally you find ways to distant yourself from God and his ways. I want to encourage you to turn it around because God has blessings in store for you that can only be done by his power.

Freedom to do anything in life away from religion has become more of an active way of life lately in the world. *YOLO* is what they call it. The word has become a phenomenon. If you are curious of the meaning of this word it means, *you only live once*. This word has become the theme of lives across the world. This is not only destroying the believer's minds, but also destroying the lives for generations. Pursuing a life filled with selfish pleasures limits our growth with God.

It is hard for us to imagine life after we die. The life you have now, are you really living? Does it feel like you just exist and you're life never amounts to anything? God has created you for a specific purpose. He wouldn't have created you if you weren't meant for something significant. You have an assignment to fulfill and he wants you to accomplish everything your heart truly desires. He promises us much more than any of our family and friends could offer. The love of God is forever and his blessings don't end when we die, but it will be greater things stored up for us in heaven. As dream pursuers we must seek the one who can bring our dreams into reality.

Twenty-Two

Love is an amazing gift from God that can be used for good or bad. The good and bad determine how you pursue certain things. Love is something that not only feels us with joy, but it motivates us to do better in life. We will do whatever it takes to keep those things we love and the things that love us. Falling in love with my high school sweet heart I knew I was going to marry her the first time I spoke to her. I knew I loved her because I couldn't see myself with anyone else besides her and I couldn't imagine her being with someone that wasn't me.

Our minds can play tricks on us when we are in love with someone. We have to make sure we guard our thoughts from negativity or lusting after others besides the one we love. There are a lot of times we lust after things, but say we love it, but find ourselves getting bored with that specific thing or person. Meeting my high school sweet heart, I knew it had to be fate because we are still together over 7 years now and we can't stay away from each other. We've had disagreements before and weren't always seeing eye to eye on things, but it was through God that showed us how to love each other. I know you say, wait until 5 years from now you probably can't wait to get away from her, but I can't see that because my love is different than yours.

My love can't be compared to others love for things because everyone loves differently. Someone who says they love their wife and still cheat on them, I wonder how then their love is defined? Even if someone says they love money and doesn't have much of it, how is their love defined? Love can be defined in so many ways and can control us to do things. Now you may be thinking, how can someone that is broke love money? It controls the person who loves it. When you love money you make decisions based off what money would do for you in that situation.

When we fall in love with the wrong thing it hinders us. Instead of falling in love with Christ, whom is love, we choose to love the things he created. We are not to worship the creation, but the creator. When we love the wrong things it can cause us to do things out of our character. When I look at the word *love* defined by Christ, it's so amazing. In the Bible it says, God so loved the world that he gave his only son. God loved us enough to allow his son to be crucified on the cross for our sins. This type of love is so huge and can't be compared. When we pursue God with our hearts he will start to fill us with the true meaning of love.

You may think I am going too far, but I believe the word has been devalued. The world tries to define what God's love is. We see exposure with money, jewelry, a huge house, nice cars, and beautiful women to sleep with, but this isn't what God is. A young rapper after getting his award wants to first thank God for his award and he goes into the rest of his list of thanking his crew, as if by thanking God first adds more value to the thank you. The world tries to connect God with all these things, so people are convinced if we don't experience that type of life than we don't know the real God. The glamour is all a show for people to envy them of the things they have.

Rappers may be thankful for their riches they have, but are they thanking God or thanking themselves for such a success they became. It's not limited to rappers, but it goes as far as pro athletes, actors, and even pastors in the church as well. We can misuse the influence of God on our lives. If it seems like we got it all together from everyone's perspectives than it's okay. I want you to desire to have a relationship with God instead of chasing the love of materialistic things.

Across America they are trying to take God out of schools. If the word of God weren't powerful the government wouldn't feel the need to take it out of schools. It's okay to learn about mythology in schools, but it's wrong to say the pledge of allegiance in class. I was never taught about Jesus in school, but I learned a lot about American history and history of mythology. If God was fake or unreal, why do they feel the need to take it out of schools? When Christianity is taught in school I learned how a lot of them were persecuted and put to death because of their faith, but never showed the benefits of being a believer. I am glad I didn't count on a teacher in school to teach me about my faith.

That was just a thought I wanted to share with you because I find it interesting how it's all happening. Now back to the amazing life God has prepared for you. I am not perfect, but there is a difference of saying we love Christ and really loving Christ through faith. The love for Christ has been devalued by our way of life because we want to enjoy what we have and do what we want instead of fully living right.

God has a plan for you. It will be times of struggle and pain, but the Lord has overcome it all for us. If we continue to stay faithful to him, he is able to do more because faith is pleasing to him. Love for Jesus doesn't end and it should be a constant growth because you should see more and more of the amazing things he's done for you. We shouldn't be motivated by what we see, but by the love he has for us to die on the Christ, which freed us from the power of sin. God so loved the *world* that he gave his only begotten son. He didn't just die for me, but he died for you too. This is the truth from God no matter what people say. He has given us another chance at life to honor him in our ways and spread his word across the world.

Twenty-Three

Today I woke up with an excited and eager spirit to pursue greater than what I can normally do on my own. Working graveyard shifts for 4 nights and 50-hour weeks, it put a toll on me. I had to get in my head that I am meant for so much more than what I was accustomed to. I saw people satisfied with getting a paycheck every two weeks, but I knew my God had so much more for me.

I believe God's process of me learning my true worth here on earth is spectacular and I couldn't have wished it to be done a better way. I don't knock anyone working in a warehouse at all or any other jobs for that matter, but I came to a conclusion of knowing I can do all things through Christ. He will humble us to prepare us for our future. I know God was still preparing me for something better. I now am prepare for his favor wherever I go because I know God wants more for me.

Everything that you go through is for a reason. You can either let battles defeat you or can allow it to uplift you. Many of times in my life I was let down, treated badly, and laughed at by so many people and if you know what I mean you understand the pain and struggles you go through in the process of discovering your purpose. It's hard to trust others with your dreams, so you guard your heart from people. You don't want them to know exactly your real dreams because you think they will look at you differently. I want to say that God placed that dream in your heart for a reason and it is meant for you to fulfill it. I know it seems impossible sometimes because you don't know how it's going to happen, but your job is to keep your faith in Christ and believe that it will be done no matter how it looks.

You may be working a job that you really want to quit, but you have kids and bills to pay. You can still pursue what you're passionate about, but it's just going to require more work on your part. You must seek God and ask how you can make the dream happen for you to get you out of the circumstances you are experiencing right now. I understand the thinking of giving up on a dream because it seems too hard or impossible, but you cant give up on the dream. That dream is connected to your purpose in life. Some of your family may not agree with it, but God placed that desire in your heart for a reason and you must obey him and dedicate your life to giving it your best.

You may be experiencing some troubles right now, but your expectations will not only push you to your dreams, but you will do more than you even thought you were capable of doing. You can trust in the Lord that he will help you keep a vision for yourself. When we put all the weight on our shoulders we don't give God a chance to work his favor in our lives the way he wants. When you trust in God, do the part you can and allow him to do the rest. You are no capable of doing everything on your own. He wants you to rely on him so that he can work through your life. The things you know you should do on your own do them and God will handle the rest.

I heard an amazing song by Hilsong called, I Surrender. This song really spoke to me because it was the exact issue I was dealing with at the time of me hearing it. I heard this song plenty of times, but it was this time that I really understood the meaning of the words. I couldn't seem to fully surrender myself to God in some areas of my life because I enjoyed some parts I didn't want God to mess with. I wanted him to overlook that part in my life as if it wasn't wrong and still bless me no matter what. I wanted to keep my own little dirt. I tried letting go, but it seemed to get harder.

I needed to completely surrender my life over to God because I was racking my brain wondering why this certain issue still keeps showing up. The song helped me listen to God no matter what it looks like in my life. I can depend on him in the toughest situations of my life. I know it can be tough sometimes when you physically can't see something better happening, but faith is seeing it done without it actually being done yet. It means believing without seeing. It is trusting in a God that you can't see right in front of you, but you believe he lives inside you.

I know it can be hard to depend on a God that you can't see. The norm is to do things on your own and struggle. You have to believe far beyond the norm. God doesn't work miracles on how it's supposed to be done. Scientist cannot prove miracles. Scientist tries hard to explain the creation of the world because they want to prove that it isn't God. Instead of struggling to make ends meet and handle things on your own, God wants you to have faith in him that he will take care of your every need. His word never lies and when you put into practice his word, your faith will grow.

You may have tried believing for a week or a month and you're losing your faith because nothing happened. I want you to believe through that stage of when doubts come. Doubts will come. Stand firm in faith and trust that God has taken care of you. You have to praise God in advance before you can even see your blessing. Those dreams that you are pursuing are not for you, but it's connected to change someone else's life.

When he created you he could have given all your desires to someone else, but he didn't. He gave those specific dreams to you because he knew who you would become. Even when all you heard growing up was that you will never amount to anything. Believe the truth God says about you. You are more than a conqueror. No weapon formed against you shall prosper. The Lord will fill your days with prosperity. The favor of God surrounds you like a shield. Psalms 34 says, *"we may experience many troubles, but the Lord has delivered us out of them all"*. There was nothing left out of this text when he said all things.

He is filling you with creative ideas that you're passionate about to build the kingdom of God. Don't give up on those dreams. Believe that God will restore your strength so nothing will stop you from your destiny. You may go to bed feeling exhausted and beaten down, but believe that God is restoring your strength. His righteousness reigns in you. If you have believed for some big dreams to happen for you I want you to thank God in advance for him bringing your dreams into reality. It is only a matter of time before you will start living out the dream God placed in your heart

Twenty-Four

I like reading a lot in the book of proverbs. It has changed my perception of God's divine beauty. The purpose of this book in the Bible was to teach wisdom, discipline, and a prudent life. I didn't expect to be challenged in my walk with God. I began to see how much junk I had in my life and how much I needed God. I faced more challenges to test my faith. In order for me to be successful in life I need to know that I can depend on God in every downfall. Without his grace it will be impossible for me to stay on his path. When you pursue desires God placed in your heart your past tries to remind of what you use to be. The past can never tell you what you're going to be, but it'll always tell you who you use to be.

There may have been time in your life when you tried to pursue something bigger than you and fear stopped you in your tracks. When you pursue something bigger than you, God's wisdom is a must because without his it our minds are weak. We sometimes believe we know it all. We think we're grown and we can do whatever we want to do.

When you step on the path God has for you then you will be challenged in a lot of areas in your life. The book of proverbs is interesting to me and helps me see God's will being done in my life. Without knowing his word it would be impossible for me to see it. Without his wisdom you could think that people just don't want you to make it, or you think you need to change your career, but you must understand God directs you on your paths.

If you are just living and doing your own thing, who do you think is directing your steps? Is it you or God? When we make choices based off his wisdom and go through problems it's easier to understand that it's time to stay in faith. We must run after God's wisdom and if you have gotten to a place where you feel you're grown and you don't need someone telling you what to do. Just expect a big slap in the face when things go wrong. God's wisdom doesn't compare with street smarts. Wisdom from God related a lot to street smart because it's not taught in school or in the Bible. Wisdom from God is taught by experience and also seeing others experiencing something as well and you learn from it.

It's good to know scriptures but it's different when you live it. You have a different perspective on the word. I know people who can memorize scriptures, but what's the point of memorizing it if you don't live it? Satan even knows God's word, but that doesn't ensure him success to be in heaven. The fear of God is the beginning of knowledge.

We are slaves to either two things, a slave to sin or a slave to righteousness. Slave to sin is when we allow our fleshly desires to control us. You think you're not a slave to it because you don't do it that much, but that is a trap the enemy wants you to believe. We think like this all the time because we don't want to feel like we're those people in the world killing, stealing, and living a life of sin. No matter how big or small the sin is to us, God despises all sin. When we obey the flesh that means we are slaves to sin. If we as believers are slaves to righteousness then this means we obey the things of God. The good news about this is you don't have to be angry with me because I have courage enough to say it, but you can make a decision to change. We were all slaves of sin before Christ, but we can now live through his righteousness.

You say to yourself, God loves me for who I am. This is true. He does love you, but he also loves you enough to push you to grow so you can experience everything he has for you. How do you think God feels when you use him just to get a blessing? I know this sounds terrible, but our minds work like this if we are not rooted in the word of God. When is it going to be time for us to surrender to him and seek His wisdom so we can live the way he wants us to? We could change now, but we have a lot of things to take care of first. We want to wait until we get more settled in life then we can focus on God more.

Don't choose to serve God when it's convenient for you. It isn't the way to go and when you choose this route you are no longer operating by his favor. I want to encourage you to see that obeying God can be tough sometimes, but the reward is so much greater than what our minds can imagine. God can do all things. He is the only one that can free you of that bondage you have dealt with in your life for so long. That little voice inside of you wants to obey God, but the anger and bitterness inside of you is keeping you away from

Him. If you come to know God more and seek his wisdom, he is able to take that burden off your shoulders.

We all have a purpose of our existence. The answers to our questions are in the hands of our Lord. You have made decisions in your life you felt was good enough, but God needs you to sacrifice more for him. He doesn't do this to cause pain, but he does it for your gain. It's not impossible to live in peace because your peace rests in the Lord. Allow him to live through you so you can live your purpose.

Twenty-Five

The process of growth can be challenging sometimes. During growth we hardly focus on the end result, because the difficulty is more noticeable. Take your eyes off the pain and focus on the growth that is happening. God's wisdom doesn't always make us happy in the moment because our flesh wants to do something different. We get can frustrated with life because it gets too difficult. We begin to doubt if it's God taking us through the process or is it just our own ambitions that drive us to succeed or fail. The knowledge that needs to be learned in the process will come at a more affected rate when we lean on his understanding.

I had plenty of time to think of the good and bad things that were in my life working in places I'm not passionate about. The enemy is constantly trying to destroy my hope I have for a better life. I knew working on the assembly line wasn't for me, but it was something temporary in my life until God opened something better for me. The most challenging part for me was that I just did not know what God wanted me to do. I would ask God to tell me what I need to do. I was tired of the boring life I had and I knew I was gifted to do more, I just didn't know what it was.

In my past instead of seeking his kingdom first I chose to do what I wanted because that's what made me feel good. When I learned to put God first it made the confusing part of my life more enjoyable. We can have dreams and goals that are so big we put them before God. Constantly think about the word of God in those times of uncertainty because the enemy uses those times to get you distracted. You can't give up and especially during the times when you feel that you can't handle all the pressure. Instead of worrying and being afraid of the future, trust in God. He will never leave you alone.

It might have been times when you felt alone, but God is always there with you. I recently got my motorcycle license. It was fun and exciting, but challenging at times. If my instructor stayed alongside of me the whole time I would never learn to ride on my own. If I wanted to know how to be a good and safe rider I had to practice on my own. He never left me during my test or the class, but he watched incase I needed help. God does the same way for you. When he teaches you a lesson it's for a reason. God teaches you because you may have to face that problem down the line or help someone with the same problem. You may feel that you're alone in the struggle, but he is there watching incase you need some extra help. You have to learn how to operate in his word every day.

We will face battles as believers in Christ, but the Lord says that he has delivered us out of them all. No matter what we go through in life we can always depend on his word to pull through for us. I got a chance to live in Dornbirn,

Austria for a couple of months playing professional football. I was around the beautiful views of nature and culture I was never exposed to before. In this beautiful place there were people who don't know how American can be with violence, racism, terrorism, and any hateful act towards man. I know you would think if you lived in Europe life would be carefree. The people still live angry, stressed out, and have a life far away from Christ as much as the other country.

More than 70% of the population of this beautiful place smoked cigarettes. I even knew kids 15 and 16 years of age smoke cigarettes on the way to school. It was an okay thing out there to do. I am against something that damages my health, especially something that cuts years off my life. I am not against the people smoking, but the problems cigarettes bring on people. I want to let you know that no matter how far you go the enemy is always after you even in the most beautiful countries to live in. We must seek God wherever we go. We feel it's not bad because the Bible doesn't exactly say anything against it. It comes down to if you're willing to go beyond the norm to experience God in your life.

In God we have a purpose to live and we're not meant to go through life complaining or afraid of what other bad thing will happen. Bad things will continue happening in America. Gas will continue to go higher. Innocent people will be killed on the streets. Less people will commit themselves to God. When your faith is set firm in Christ no weapon formed against you will prosper.

Those uncomfortable times in life are great opportunities to build a relationship with Christ. When we want to have a relationship with Christ and pursue him, he can't help but open doors of opportunity. He wants us to be happy in life and enjoy the finer things, but when they mean more to you than you're relationship with him than you have to check yourself. If you been going through a tough time right now trying to figure out what's next in life it's okay. I guarantee if you pursue Christ he will begin to reveal to you desires and ways to be happy and prosperous in life. Don't give up on yourself you are closer than you think. All you have to do is reach out a hand to the Lord and he will guide your steps to victory.

Twenty-Six

You are getting close to the end of this book. I want you before reading any further to just spend a moment in prayer and thank God for all the things he has blessed you with this year. If you are sitting in a coffee shop or your room don't be ashamed to shit in quiet and reflect on his grace on your life. If you couldn't think of all the good things he did for you, just imagine what he can do for you this year. He does exceedingly, abundantly, above all we can ask or think. His favor is endless.

He has already blessed you, but it is up to you to receive his blessings. Throughout this year it will be chances you will be in to receive his blessings. If you want to grow with God it requires hard work from you to listen to him even when you want to do your own thing. It's hard sometimes because you see people around you having fun and partying and you want to do the same things. It seems painful at the moment, but the reward is so amazing and it can't compare to a night of getting high, drunk, or just having sex with a random person. You can't live off of fulfilling those fleshly desires.

In some cases there are those people who experience a near death experience and change their life around immediately. Those people are fortunate to have that opportunity because there are some who don't get that chance. The bad part about this is that we blame God because that person lost their life. That person had the choice to choose life or death and when we choose God we no longer live our own lives, but we do it through Christ. God says to die and be in heaven is gain. The plans God has for us and why things happen aren't supposed to be figured out. Some things are meant to stay known to God and we must trust that he knows best.

God says life and death is in the power of the tongue. He didn't mean this to be so confusing to us. He meant that whatever we speak over our lives daily could either bring on life or death. The rap music I use to listen could easily be applied here. We may think we're only rapping the song, but when we continue to meditate on those words and saying it, they will eventually manifest in our lives. A few of my favorite rappers are Andy Mineo, Lecrae, and Trip Lee. They are gospel rappers and talks about the truth that brings life to our dreams and purpose of living. They will continue to be successful and grow as long as they continue to do the will of God in their lives.

You may think I am a little extreme, but I feel music plays a big part in the younger generation. If my children listen to rap I want them to choose a style of rap that talks about the love of Christ in a way they understand. I use to convince myself that I could listen to any type of rap music and it'll never change me. I was stubborn, but slowly thought like the rappers I would listen to. I don't know about you, but I want to have the blessings God has for me. When those negative thoughts come up you have to speak God's word over your life. This means to trust God for what he is going to do in our life because worrying about the next day will not do any good. Don't worry about the job you applied for or a new business venture you set out to accomplish. God has you in his sight. He has not forgot about you.

If you believe in God's word you will know that this will work 100% of the time. Faith is required to get what you believe for. It's a process of growth that never ends. Thoughts of defeat are meant to break you down and cause you to give up on yourself. Only if you could imagine the things Jesus did when he was on earth. Jesus told his disciples that they would do more than what they saw him doing. He said this because after he died and rose from the dead his spirit lived in them. That same power that was in Jesus is now in you. You have the advantage to go after whatever he has placed in you and accomplish it. The only problem is we defeat ourselves by thinking we won't be able to fulfill it.

Don't think God loves a preacher more than you because he loves you the same way he loves Joel Osteen. It is just up to us if we have the faith to receive every bit of blessings he has for us. It's according to our faith that produces what we see in our lives. If you haven't been seeing positive things in your life then it's time to turn it around and believe for greater. If your life is messed up right now it's not because God did it to you. Your life is messed up for a reason. Instead of complaining, stand in faith no matter what it looks like God is turning the situation around.

Some people were raised in a home or neighborhood where surviving means killing someone who's in the wrong neighborhood. To some people selling drugs to addicts is the only way to provide for their family. It's difficult to change from a life that has been so instinctive to survive in, but God has better for you. If you want to start seeing greater things happen in your life it's time you raise that level of expectation. Jesus said if we have faith as small as a mustard seed to move a mountain and if we believe it, we will see it happen. We shouldn't put our faith in ourselves, but in Christ. We all have faced some mountains in our life and it is according to our faith if that mountain will move out the way.

Trust in God for every situation you face in life no matter how big. We sometimes have the faith for small things because we know God will do it for us. When it comes to those problems that are bigger than us, fear wants to step in. Don't allow fear to control you, but allow his word to direct your steps. Plant the seed of faith and watch how his plans for you are revealed.

Twenty-Seven

An issue that people deal with still is forgiveness. We struggle with the sin in our lives and feel that God isn't willing to forgive us for what we did. We condemn ourselves day after day from the things we did wrong because we know that it wasn't something God approved of. We deal with issues from the world that continues to hold us back from fulfilling a great relationship with Jesus. Peter asked Jesus, how many times should we forgive our enemy? Peter thought seven times was good enough. The significance for the number 7 meant *perfection,* in the eyes of the people.

Peter figured seven was good enough since it was a perfect number, how could it get better than that, right? But Jesus replied, not seven times, but seventy-seven times. Jesus meant not just seven, but continual forgiveness as he has done for us. We are quick to hate someone because they cut us off on the freeway, or someone offended us. Our forgiveness should be perfect like him so we should always forgive those who hurt us and even ourselves for wrongs we've done.

It's ridiculous when family members can be so unforgiving to each other. I know you have some in your family; I'm just brave enough to put it out there. When we hold certain things inside it can limit the growth we experience with God. If we aren't willing to forgive a cousin, nephew, uncle, aunt, father, mother and the list goes on, how do we expect to accept the forgiveness from God. When will we realize we have been completely forgiven for what we have done? We are human and mistakes come with being human. If you neglect forgiving someone, peace will never fully enter in your heart. You will continue trying to gain the acceptance from God when it has already been given. Forgiveness needs to be more exposed in family. If we allow our kids and their kids to grow up not forgiving, we train generations to not reach their full potential with God.

Our father in heaven has forgiven us even when we did wrong and we knew we were disobedient. God has forgiven you of your sins and the things you have done that are against his will for your life. You say you want to change, but you continue to live like you haven't been forgiven. The Lord has forgiven you, so now you can live a life that proves you have been forgiven. If you lie to your mom or dad and they find out you lied, it's never good for you. They may be angry and disappointed, but they forgive you of what you've done because they love you. An obedient child will make sure to not do it again.

God has forgiven you; we should be willing to forgive. Don't get me wrong I know we are human and we aren't perfect, but that's the beauty of knowing god. We don't have to live with that bitterness in our hearts. We can ask God to help us forgive that person. If you genuinely don't want to forgive that person, you can expect more bitterness to pile on to that. Is that a way a child of God should act? I am not saying God will disown you, but when you continue to live bitter you will forfeit his favor he has on you.

You can either choose to live chasing negative thoughts or you can listen to God and trust his word that he made you an overcomer. I know you don't feel like it right now because you continue messing up and having your own *in the closet* sins, but God is always there. He wants you to be free from whatever is holding you back. The enemy wants you to sulk in your shame and feel like you will never be who God wants you to be, but that's a lie. The devil is already defeated and the word of God is truth. God says you can do all things through him if you believe. You may be experiencing hell right now, but if you believe you can do all things through him, he will empower you to do so. Pursue him with all your heart and you will experience more of what he has for you. Spiraling in your shame only makes you worse and puts you down more and more and it'll seem hard to get out of it. God is giving you that ladder to climb out because he wants you to live above the enemy and not with him. That is why God placed the enemy under our feet for a reason.

Don't be afraid to stand up for Christ because you think if you get to close to God then the enemy is going to target you more. Guess what? You are a target for the enemy right now and you don't know it because you are being encouraged to do more for God. When you have been living in hell for so long the righteous path can always seem like a struggle and too much of a pain to do right now. You don't know how good you have it to make a change in other people's life. You have a gift and that gift is to be used to spread the love of Christ on the earth.

You feel living in your sin keeps you happier than when you would go to church or talk about Christ with your friends because you didn't feel so out of place. We try to imagine Christ as someone who is going to bless us no matter what we do as long as we get saved and go to church. Once we are saved the spirit of Christ lives in us and having Christ in us means we should be more like him. Making better decisions will open opportunities to experience his favor. Whatever it is, God has empowered you to do it.

It's hard for me when I come across people that say they are believers, but they don't truly believe in the word of God. They go to church on Easter Sunday and Christmas and think they are doing enough. I think the problem is we feel we want to make God happy by going to church when it counts on these big holidays and not commit to a life change of knowing him. God needs more from us as believers because purpose requires more time than a few church visits a year. You don't have to jump around shouting and screaming and speaking in tongues to know God. Church isn't the requirement from God, but he knows when we gather in church with other believers, we are empowered by each other. His spirit moves when his children are gathered in his name.

Church isn't about just hearing a message from a pastor because watching church online can easily be done. Church is about being in the presence of the Lord. It's about gathering with other believers to hear the word of God. You can't grow with God when you isolate yourself in your home and never be challenged. When you go to church you're in an environment with other hurt, abused, ignored, and depressed people. God wants to heal all those who come to be in his presence. He wants you to connect with members of the body of Christ. It is to bring him glory. Church isn't just for you, but it's for someone else who is hurt and sees no other way they will live without God. Maybe that's what it is. Are you hurting enough to only depend on God to help you?

Don't spend days wondering what you need to do in life to make it big. Deciding to live for Christ will be the greatest decision you will ever make. It will not only free you from all your downfalls, but his presence will enable you to do more than you planned in life. Without faith it is impossible to please God. Good deeds don't please God. Even going to church doesn't please God if it isn't followed by acts of obedience. When you operate in faith, you please God. Having faith in him will open doors that no person can shut. I know God has placed a gift inside of you to change the world. Stop getting down on yourself and blaming other people for the life you live because God can turn it around for you. It isn't too late to fulfill the purpose God has for you.

Twenty-Eight

For years people struggle in life to fulfill the purpose they were created for. The pattern starts at the beginning of the year. New gym memberships, new diet plans, big goals, anything that gives the feeling of a fresh start. Something small happens and throws you totally off your game. Without obeying God and going after the dreams he placed in our hearts we will not grow the way he wants. Life is too short to give up on dreams. We have to be more confident in God that he is going to do what his word says. Faith is a scary thing. If it were easy to live by faith I know everyone would do it.

When we set our ways on the teachings of God, no matter the ups and downs we face, defeat can't be an option. The problem for us is when we encounter problems we get shaken up, stressed out, and complain how tough life is or how much we hate where we work. You can continue to complain and stress every day, but until you start speaking truth from God, nothing will change.

God doesn't ignore our issues because he works on the solution before the problem arises. The struggle was never meant to break you down, but it was always meant to build you up. We all go through stressful times, but your faith can determine how long you stay in that season of struggle. I think bigger now because I know God can afford my dreams. If you think your dreams are to big for God, you are wrong. I remember sitting in my room one day in tears. I was angry because I didn't think I was ever going to accomplish my dreams. I didn't understand my reason for living and what I was created to do. If you came to a point in your life like I did I hope you know you're not alone.

If you have been going through treatments for cancer and you feel you are going to die at a young age, don't believe it. God can do all things and if you truly believe God is your healer, continue to trust in the Lord to heal you. I am in agreement that God will show himself on your behalf and work a miracle in you.

Don't meditate on one negative thought of death because the enemy wants you to focus on your situation. Psalm 103 explains how God has forgiven you of your sins and heals all diseases. Keep the joy of the Lord in your heart because laughter is like medicine to the body and strength to the spirit. God has placed so much in you and he wants you to understand the things you can accomplish. If you have dreams to be an astronaut, it's not impossible. If you want to be President of the United States one day, it's possible. If you want to be a professional athlete, believe you are going to be one. If you want to be married with kids that love the Lord, it's possible. It starts with you moving in the right direction no matter how difficult it looks. The Lord is with you every step of the way. He will protect us. Are you willing to leave behind what has no value to the kingdom of God to pursue him more?

There is going to be some extra baggage in your life that will be left back because God will need to cut it off for you to reach your purpose. Friends you use to kick it with before may not stick around anymore. You can't allow extra baggage to slow you down. Matthew 19:28-30 says *"A person who leaves his brother, sister, mother, father, or wife to pursue Christ has treasures stored up for them in heaven"*. I don't know about you, but I am willing to risk it all to encounter a greater relationship with my Lord. I know you may have doubts, but just take that step of faith.

Twenty-Nine

Atime will come in your life when you feel you can't give anymore. You're just tired of the problems in your life and you just want to escape it all. You have worked so hard to live for God and you haven't been seeing the results that you wanted. You been praying for a new job and now a situation has come up that is going to cost you some money. You may have been planning to do things this year, but financially you haven't been able to do it. You may have said you were going to do something to start a business or go back to school, but procrastination steps in and you still haven't got it done. It gets tough in life sometimes when you have a dream in your heart and you give everything towards it and nothing seems to happen.

It is time to take it to another level with your faith. When you get worn down spiritually God is there to be your strength. If you remain in the Lord, he is faithful to you. When you have been drained and life seems to attack you just release it to God because he has all the answers. You have lived at such a low level for so long it is easy to expect less because you don't think good things will happen anymore for you. You can't go through life on autopilot just hoping that God will bless you with a million dollars. Settling in life shouldn't be an option for you.

People give up on dreams. When times get rough make sure to stand firm in faith and never give up on that dream. We say we want a better relationship with God, but we're still living in darkness. Living in darkness doesn't mean you just smoke weed, gangbang, or have sex with a lot people, but to live away from the light of Christ means you are in darkness. Walking by faith you may not know exactly where to go, but that faith keeping you in the light will eventually bring those dreams and desires into reality.

God will allow you to live the way you want and he doesn't force salvation on you. If you want to live away from him don't blame it on him when it goes bad. I use to do it myself. I wanted to live my way and do what I wanted, but when things were unsuccessful I would be angry towards God. You don't have to worry about someone stopping you from the blessings of God. God loves you and gives you freedom to choose what to believe in. His purpose for your life is not going to be boring and stupid. God's plan for you is connected to his reason for creating earth.

You determine your future not everyone else. If every one determined my future I would just go around asking people what I should do in life and stick to whatever they say. You might have been living a lie so long that you are convinced that what you're doing is helping out people. Scientist has proven facts of marijuana helping certain diseases. God understands the influence of marijuana in people's lives. Does smoking weed once in a while hurt?

That's not me to decide. I know what it does and doesn't do for me. It alters my mind of true faith in God with a lie. It convinces me that I don't have to live by faith to enjoy life. Why deal with stress of the world when I can just smoke a little to take the edge off? When we do this, it never develops our faith. We rely more on what time of strand is going to get me high other than believing God for my breakthrough.

God created all things, but man chooses to use marijuana as a gateway to escape the pressure of life instead of dealing with life by putting their trust in God. People even believe they are smarter when they smoke weed. They don't gain the true knowledge of God. God is your source of healing. Don't give up on your faith to depend on some weed to provide you with all the answers of life.

It is almost the end of this book and I want you to understand that I don't look down on anyone. I want you to experience more of what God has for you. Eliminate whatever is damaging your faith in Christ. I understand it is a process, but to begin that process you have to start moving in the right direction. He is the healer to your diseases, your pain, your suffering, your fears, your failures, your worries, or anything else in life that's much bigger than you. I don't reject doctors because they are needed, but don't put your life in the hands of doctors who can't give you life the way Christ has already done. I know family members who had cancer and beat it because they depended on the word of God and not what a doctor's diagnosis said. You can't lean on the word if you don't know it.

You will experience miracles doctors can't explain. Financial breakthroughs you can't explain how it happened. It is so much more God has promised through His word.

You don't have to be intimidated by how the world operates because being a believer; we operate by a different system that doesn't operate with the ways of this world. The way God does things can't be explained by science all the time. If you are tired of wasting years of not fulfilling your purpose, God is with you reaching his hand out. He wants you to be fulfilled in this earth. You may not see it now, but he is already working on your problems. When you allow Christ to live through you, the ways of the righteous will be made known by your faith.

Be persistence of speaking life over every situation. Don't allow negative thoughts come out your mouth.

"Blessed is the one who does not walk in step with the wicked or stand in the way that sinners take or sit in the company of mockers, but whose delight is in the Lord, and who meditates on his word day and night. That person is like a tree planted in the streams of water, which yields its fruit in season and whose leaf does not wither and whatever they do prospers." –Psalms 1

When you meditate on the things of God prosperity abounds in you. You know that when you meditate on the things of God you will prosper. When you pursue God you will get direction to where you need to go in your next steps in life. You may not know what you desire or maybe the things you love isn't what God intends for you, but when you pursue heart of Christ, he will place desires in your heart and his plans for you will be done.

Thirty

You have made it to the end of this book and I just want to say thank you for this great opportunity of allowing me to encourage you throughout these 30 days. When we struggle it pushes us to grow and forces us to rise above our problems. When you act in fear with those struggles instead of faith it makes it harder to receive your breakthrough. Nothing limits his power from going forth in the earth. I know he has placed desires in your heart to serve him in so many ways that you will love. He has given you gifts and desires to pursue a certain career or dream.

If you been a certain way for so long don't give up on yourself to think you will never change. Trust in the Lord that you will find your way out of that destructive mindset. We have all sinned and none of us are perfect, only our Lord and Savior Jesus Christ. You may not feel like Jesus lives in you because of the way your life is right now, but he does. Surround yourself with people who will encourage you to live more for God, instead of chasing a lifestyle the world desires. Once Jesus died on the cross and rose again, he proved that the enemy is defeated. I serve only one God and no other thing can compare to the love that exist in Christ.

When I need help I can always depend on God's promises and you can do the same. I know during the time of reading this book you have been challenged in your life to give up some things that you want to hold on to. When you commit yourself to God, you will need less of the things that use to bring you pleasure. He wants you to live less for yourself, so that he can be more in your life. You may finish this book and think it was good, but reality isn't that easy. When you operate by the word of God, *reality,* as you know it doesn't apply to you anymore.

Without faith it is impossible to please God. We are put to the test every day when we wake up. We can either decide to live by faith or doubt. I pray this book has changed your life. Encouragement is something we all need to stay focused on God's purpose for our lives. Ask God to bring those encouragers you need to push you to the next level in your faith.

I want you to live a life of abundance and impacting lives every day by the spirit of the Lord working through you. I know you will fulfill your dreams when you pursue the heart of Christ. No more sleepless nights worrying about this or that, but you will begin to experience God waking you up earlier because you can't wait to go after the things he has for you.

Closing

My journey of finding Christ was never perfect. I struggled with many things growing in my faith. I never judge those who struggle in their faith because I understand how tough it is to obey God in this world. Temptation is all around us and God understands what we go through. If you trust in the Lord with all your heart and depend on his wisdom to make it through your struggles, he will never fail. He loves his people too much to not give us a great assignment here on earth.

You are going to face some struggling times in life. It's what you do during those moments of difficulty that defines who you are as a believer in Christ. I wish it was an easy way of living, but it requires faith. The reward of honoring God is life. God isn't good to you because you're rich or have everything money can buy. God is good because what he did on the cross. He gives you peace and prosperity in every step when you trust in him. It's by his grace you are able to do what you do.

I want to thank my parents Felix and Elaine Bobo. Two powerful leaders in the body of Christ and has kept me close to God even when I tried to live my own life. My three siblings, Felix, Reyshawn, and Cherisa continued to help me grow as a brother and a follower in Christ. My bride to be, Maya Curtis, you are an inspiration. You make me a better man and I thank God I met someone like you. I want to thank my family and friends who have been part of my life because I am inspired by all of you.

I thank God for this opportunity to write my first book to encourage you to believe that attaining a higher life is achievable when you obey the word of God. I pray that God will do amazing things in your life as you pursue him in all your ways. Don't give up when life gets difficult. Keep your vision in front of you. You are created to be a life changer in your home, neighborhood, city, state, wherever you go. God will use you in many ways, if you allow him. Nothing is impossible through Christ.

Printed in the United States
By Bookmasters